HABITUAL DOMAINS

Also by Po-Lung Yu, Ph.D.

Forming Winning Strategies:
An Integrated Theory of Habitual Domains
(in English)

Multiple Criteria Decision-Making:
Concepts, Techniques and Extensions
(in English)

The Universal Bag of Wisdom
(in Chinese)

Reaching for a Higher State of Wisdom
(in Chinese)

Knowing People and Making Strategical Decisions
(Co-authored with S.D. Huang in Chinese; a Chinese
National Book Award winner)

New States of Mind and Behavior —
Theory and Application
(in Chinese)

Behavior Mechanisms and Strategical Decisions:
The Foundation of Knowing Yourself and Others
(in Chinese)

Praise For Habitual Domains

"Business success today is built on teamwork and communication. But those traits exist only with the kind of self-knowledge that Habitual Domains will help you find."

> — Burnell R. Roberts
> Former Chairman and CEO, The Mead Corporation

"Habitual Domains offers you all the tools you need to build a productive team and to organize a creative workforce among people with vastly different cultural backgrounds. Using HD, I have led Sunrise Department Store to success. I turned the store around from big losses to handsome profit in one year."

> — Alex R. Ferng
> President, Sunrise Department Store
> Shanghai, China

"The application of the concept of habitual domains gave China Steel its key to success."

> — Mou-Hui King
> Chairman (retired), China Steel Corporation
> Kaohsiung, Taiwan

"Habitual Domains is a great concept which has transformed my life and business. I personally practice the concepts of HD and believe it makes me a more effective and wiser person."

> — Judy M. L. Chen
> President of Tah Tong Battery Company
> Taipei, Taiwan

To inquire about Dr. Po-Lung Yu's lectures, seminars or audiotapes, please contact
JMA, Inc., P.O. Box 30116,
Kansas City, Missouri 64112

HABITUAL DOMAINS

Freeing Yourself From the Limits on Your Life

by

Po-Lung Yu, Ph.D.
With a Foreword by Paul H. Henson

Highwater Editions

First Edition
Published in 1995

Copyright © Po-Lung Yu, Ph.D. 1995

Photographs © Roy Inman or Joe Parker, or used with permission

The material in Appendix 2, pages 182-188, was previously published on pages 266-272 in
Forming Winning Strategies: An Integrated Theory of Habitual Domain by P.L.Yu,
©1990 Springer-Verlag GmbH & Co. The author gratefully acknowledges permission
to use this material.

 Habitual Domains® is a registered trademark

ISBN 0-932-845-70-3

Library of Congress Catalog Number 95-76547
(CIP Data available)

Published by Highwater Editions, Shawnee Mission, Kansas
Printed and bound in the United States of America

Dedication

To all the people who made it possible
for you to read this book now,
and to all people who understand,
practice and share the concepts
of Habitual Domains,
so as to make themselves happier and wiser,
and society better.

Foreword

The concept of Habitual Domains explained in this book changed my life. I believe it can change others' lives for the better, too. I am certain it can change the corporate culture in our country, probably as much as Total Quality Management (TQM) and with considerably more benefit to individuals within corporations.

Although the American business marketplace needs the productivity boost these ideas can bring, I doubt that Habitual Domains will attain the buzzword status of TQM (and many other good ideas). Habitual Domains has far too much common sense for that.

We Americans love a speedy solution to just about everything. We've given the world the concept and reality of "instant" gratification. From instant oatmeal to the instant replay to "Just In Time" inventory, we've learned a lot of ways to get what we want quickly.

Yet even with all these ready responses to many of our needs, most of us still crave something we can't get in a hurry.

We want meaning.

We want to know who we are and why we matter in the greater scheme of things. We want a sense of purpose and value. I think most people believe that a greater truth exists beyond the culture of busyness that we've built. Deep down, we suspect there's more to life than what we are experiencing. Deep down we know we are capable of far more than is asked of us. But we feel powerless to discover that greater truth ourselves.

How do we find out what is really there? For me, Habitual Domains makes a lot of sense.

My interest in Habitual Domains began with a purely business motive. I first turned to Dr. Po-Lung Yu for the kind of counsel many businesses around the world have looked to him to find — advice on operations issues, strategy and models for decision-making inside a corporation.

It was an easy choice. I knew firsthand of Dr. Yu's brilliance in many fields of endeavor. In 1977, the University of Kansas selected Dr. Yu to hold the chair as the Carl A. Scupin Distinguished Professor of Business. I had helped establish this chair in honor of "Skip" Scupin, my friend and my mentor in the telecommunications business.

Dr. Yu was only 36, the youngest professor ever to hold a distinguished professorship at the university. But what a unique mix of talents he brought to academia and business! He is a Phi Beta Kappa, Ph.D. industrial engineer, operations strategist, Kung Fu master and calligrapher, who wins coveted teaching awards. And he farms, besides.

He is an extraordinary thinker, teacher and business strategist, but he also brings to every encounter a timeless wisdom and generosity of spirit. Part of what distinguishes Habitual Domains from other systems of self-discovery is the wise and caring voice of a man who draws upon the ways of both East and West and whose own life is a wonderful example of the ideas he is explaining.

It was exactly that set of traits I found within Habitual Domains, the system of thought and action he has developed over the years.

Certainly it is a management tool, and a powerful one at that. As you will see, the concept of Habitual Domains in business operates on several levels vital to the health of an organization.

But Habitual Domains may be most fundamentally valuable as a way to realize the full capabilities of the people working in America today.

Every business knows that its business success depends on its people. Yet every company also knows to its frustration that the potential of its people remains largely untapped. How vast would success be if the people of a company were realizing their full potential? The effect on quality, excellence, change for growth and profitability would be enormous.

Habitual Domains can help that happen. Slowly, but surely.

This is not a book about quick fixes. It is a book about personal and organizational growth and a way of thinking that is meant to last a lifetime.

The concept of Habitual Domains has made a positive difference for me. I believe it can do the same for you and for anyone who wants to break through the limits life seems to impose. I recommend it to you with gratitude for your interest and a promise that you will find something here to value.

Paul H. Henson
Chairman, Kansas City Southern Industries

Contents

Author's Preface and Acknowledgments

I have been a very fortunate person to initiate the study of Habitual Domains (HD). The concept began to take form in 1977 and gradually became a system of thought by 1985, including its mathematical development.

Before 1985, I focused on my writing and publication for academicians, who constitute less than one percent of the human population. Then, I began to question, Why should such a good thing as HD concepts only be read and understood by academicians? How about the 99 percent of the population I had neglected?

This thought prompted me to begin to write more easily understandable books so that I could reach more people and possibly touch their lives in positive ways. I have even produced a book about Habitual Domains that is entirely in cartoon form. Busy executives in Taiwan and China have said they like it very much because it makes study and review so easy.

I have been lucky that many people, most of them corporate executives, have subscribed readily to the concepts of HD and have helped me share the ideas. The students who have taken my short courses or lectures have formed HD clubs in Taiwan, China and Malaysia, to help disseminate HD concepts, to help themselves and to help society.

The concept of Habitual Domains is incredibly simple, but the results you can experience from using this concept are complex and transforming, and they range widely across all aspects of life.

The incredibly simple basis for HD is this: Each of you has within you the power to free yourselves from limits on your lives — limits that can keep you from realizing your dreams; limits that hold you apart from other people, even those you love; limits that bind you to a smaller sphere of success than you deserve. Freeing yourself is a decision you can make, once you understand enough about yourself to see clearly what you really want and to commit to a decision to go for it.

Our Habitual Domains affect virtually every arena of our lives. If we can only expand our Habitual Domains (or HDs), we can improve our performance at work, in social situations and in our interactions with others. By understanding and restructuring our habits, really our human software, we will be better prepared to solve problems, make decisions, resolve conflicts and crises and achieve our goals in relationships, career management and community leadership.

This is not to say your life will be without problems. No life is. But you will bring to the problems a spirit of inquiry that will allow you to see solutions and to enjoy the process of solving the problems.

The process of exploring your habitual domain will create in your life a restoration of balance and a sense of harmony. You will be filled with peaceful determination. *Determination* because you will know that by your own drive, you can succeed. *Peaceful* because you will understand that in expanding your domain, you cannot fail.

This is not a solitary endeavor. Be sure to share what you have learned with others. By teaching others you give yourself the opportunity to learn, to organize systematically what you've imagined and experienced. As a result, you'll retrieve and utilize these concepts more effectively.

And please share your experiences and discovery with me. I want to learn from you.

Please enjoy yourself as you work through this book. It is a joyful process, and you will never be the same after you have begun it. You'll be better.

J am grateful to many people. I am just an observer. All that I have learned, seen and written was initially taught by my parents, teachers, friends, students and a large number of scholars and writers who set down their observations. In this regard, let me first salute all the scholars and writers who have painstakingly recorded their findings and observations, which have helped me view life and our world better.

Next let me thank a large number of teachers, colleagues, friends, and previous students. They have made my life more meaningful and enjoyable. The experiences with them have greatly enriched my life and helped my work in research and in writing this book. If there are any mistakes in this book, however, I take full responsibility.

Now, let me thank numerous people who helped me complete this book. First, my wholehearted thanks go to Mr. Paul H. Henson, chairman of Kansas City Southern Industries and retired chairman of Sprint. He is my great mentor and friend, who continuously inspires me and helps me reach a higher level of my potential. My thanks also go to Mr. William T. Esrey, chairman, Sprint, for his encouragement and support of my work on Habitual Domains.

Next, I am much obliged to Dr. Jane Mobley. She put her great talents and effort to convert my original draft of HD to the current form, which is much more lively and easier to read than before. She has been like a great general directing her associates on this project, including Robert Butler who brought a bright style to the text; Michael DeMent and Paul Peterson who further refined it; and Vivian Strand who made the beautiful design.

My original draft of the book, which is a bit technical, was based on my publications and public lectures. It was helped and edited by my friends and colleagues at the University of Kansas, especially M.E. Hall, W.W. Hui, U.K. Chong, M. McGinnis and R. League.

In my home base, I owe thanks to many of my colleagues and students, especially to the following professors: J. Charnes, K. Cogger, D. Datta, S. Hillmer, D. Karney, K. Mackenzie, L. Sherr and P. Shenoy, for their encouragement and support. I am especially grateful to Dean J. Bauman and Associate Dean V. K. Narayanan for their continued support and encouragement for my research.

My thanks also go to the following people who are especially helpful in practicing and sharing HD concepts with me: Professor T.P. Deng, L.M. Huang, D. Zhang and my brother Po-Lu; the colleagues at Hong Education and Culture Foundations: C.C. Hong, J. Lyn, T. Yang, J.M. Chan, C.C.

Yang,and M.L. Chang; Dr. C. Shih from China Productivity Center; the executive members of the Taiwan HD Club: T.Y. Kuo, C.M. Wang, W.J. Wu, P.Z. Chang, W.H. Chang, J.M.L. Chen, Y.T. Deng, J.S.Y. Kao, Y.M. Liau, A.R. Ferng, G.K.C. Ho, Y.T.M. Huang, H.R. Lin, K.M. Lin, K.S. Lin and J.Y. Shiau; M.H. King and C.Y. Wang of China Steel, Inc.; the friends of Home Dynamics of Malaysia: J.T. Wah, T.H. Tan; my friends K.S. Ang, C. Wrather and many more.

In addition, I owe special gratitude to the following scholars: S.J. Chan of IBM Santa Teresa Laboratory, C.C. Chang of Nanyang Technological University (Singapore), H.C. Chang of National Taiwan University (Taiwan), T. Gal of Fernuniversität (Germany), Y.Y. Haimes of the University of Virginia, S.D. Huang of Jiaozuo Mining Institute (China), G. Leitmann of the University of California at Berkeley, H.L. Li and G.H. Tzeng of National Chiao Tung University (Taiwan), V.W. Liu of Central Investment Holding Company (Taiwan), A. Miele of Rice University, H.J. Miser; H. Moskowitz of Purdue University, H. Nakayama of Konan University (Japan), H.D. Ratliff of Georgia Institute of Technology, Y. Sawaragi of Japan Institute of Systems Research (Japan), P. Serafini of Università degli studi di Udine (Italy), R.M. Soland of George Washington University, J. Spronk of Erasmus Universiteit, Rotterdam (Netherlands), E. Takeda and Y. Tabata of Osaka University (Japan), H.Y. Wan, Jr. of Cornell University, F.S. Wang of Union Insurance Company (Taiwan). T.S. Yu of Chung-Hua Institution of Economic Research (Taiwan), M. Zeleny of Fordham University at Lincoln Center, the late M. H. Hepp of Denison University and the late R. Isaacs of Johns Hopkins University.

Finally, I am very grateful to my wife Chao-Tzu and my daughters Lily and Lita. They provide me with cheerful support to my work spiritually and physically. I am so lucky to have them. They give me help willingly and allow me ample time to focus on my work.

In this book, I have used a number of well-known stories, of which the authors are unknown to me. To them, I would like to send my sincere thanks and my apology because I cannot give them proper credit here.

P. L. Yu

Introduction

Expanding and understanding your habitual domain is a lifelong process of self-discovery and personal growth that will make you a happier, wiser and more effective person. What is your habitual domain? It is the human software that directs the function of the most marvelous computer — your brain.

Not even the most sophisticated supercomputer can operate without the right software. The same is true for the human brain. Our "software," though, is written and rewritten daily, beginning with the memories and thinking patterns we were born with and modified by the experiences and learning we acquire in life.

I imagine this human software as a kind of bounded domain, and I call it the "habitual domain." Just as a computer's software periodically needs to be upgraded if a computer is to be used effectively, so our human software must be expanded if we are to realize our potential.

Our habitual domains affect virtually every aspect of our lives. If we can only expand our habitual domains (or HDs) we can improve our performance at work, in social situations and in our interactions with others. By understanding and restructuring our habitual domain, really our human software, we will be better prepared to solve problems, make decisions, resolve conflicts and crises, and achieve our goals in relationships, career management and community leadership.

Nor are habitual domains a matter only of personal concern. Corporations have their own habitual domains. So do entire industries and even nations. And the same principles that apply to an individual HD can be used to enlarge the HDs — and thus the potential achievements — of large groups of people.

What keeps us from expanding our domains? Habits. We are bound by the habits we choose or allow to develop during our learning experiences. Paradoxically, we select these habits because they make our learning more efficient. Like computers, our brains will find the most efficient way to use information.

Without our even being aware of it, however, our thoughts, behaviors and perceptions grow increasingly limited by these habits. These habits create a particular program in our mental computer, a program that can prevent us from using our full capabilities.

Our capabilities are truly unlimited. The human brain has 100 billion neurons. These neural cell bodies can encode and store information in virtually endless combinations, even more combinations than the most powerful computer. All that limits the combinations any one of us can create is the extent to which we have the experience, learning and will to develop our brain power. Once we can believe how true this is, we can begin to realize our fullest capabilities.

To make an enormous difference in our lives, we don't need to make much change. A very small increment can represent huge success. Remember a football team needs only to be better by one point to win a Superbowl!

Think what a difference only one percent of additional brain power could make. Studies show only about 10 percent of human neural cells are actively working at any time. What if you could add one percent? That would be one billion neurons! Can you imagine what this much more brain power could do for you? The rewards would be enormous in every area of your life.

Breaking Out of Habitual Thinking

Most of us are so fenced in to our habitual domains that we can't tap much of our potential brain power. But it is clearly possible to expand that domain to take in new possibilities. In every age, in every field of endeavor, some individuals break through their habitual behavior and ways of thinking to turn new pages in human history.

Let me give you an example. It is obvious to all of us that an apple loosened from a tree branch will fall to the ground. That fact was as apparent to prehistoric man as it is to 20th-century students in a physics class.

Still, it wasn't until nearly the 18th century that Sir Isaac

Newton asked, "What keeps the apple from flying up into the sky instead?" Contemplating that question, he formulated his law of gravitational pull.

Newton was able to "discover" gravity because he broke the boundary of habitual thinking that had dominated human thought about apples and other falling objects up to that point. His idea changed the way the world was regarded.

Let's look at an example of this kind of thinking in the business world. As we entered the 20th century it was a widely held belief — a habitual belief — that products of higher quality must always carry a higher price tag.

Henry Ford took a different approach, when he asked: "Why can't we produce automobiles that are not only of high quality but also inexpensive, so that everyone can enjoy one?"

Pondering that question led Ford to invent techniques of mass production and standardization that spawned the automobile revolution. He broke through the boundary of habitual thinking, not only enriching himself, but benefiting society in the process.

Here is another story, one I like especially, because it shows that expanding our own habitual domain can help expand others' domains and improve the potential of a group. This has immediate and important application to business and to other areas of endeavor where we interact with people.

In 1929, because of an economic depression in Japan, the successful Matsushita Company faced the prospect of laying off employees or going bankrupt. Like other companies, Matsushita's orders from sales required only 50 percent of production time to fill. The usual way to solve the problem Matsushita was facing would have been to make fewer products — requiring fewer jobs. The staff suggested cutting half the employees to save the company.

Mr. Konosuke Matsushita, owner of the company, called his staff members together and asked them this: Why not structure a working situation that would create 100 percent survivability of the company without laying off employees or cutting benefits?

He suggested an approach completely outside the habitual domain of most companies: He offered the possibility that people who were usually producers also become salespeople.

The retiring chief executive officer of a large corporation narrowed the search for his successor down to two candidates. Both individuals — candidate A and candidate B — were invited to the CEO's ranch. When he met them, he held two horses by the reins.

"Candidate A, I'm giving you this brown horse," the CEO announced. "Candidate B, you get the spotted horse. I now want you to race to the far end of the meadow and back. The person whose horse is slowest will be the next CEO of the company."

The two candidates stood there for a moment in stunned silence. They could understand a race in which the object was to be the fastest — but the slowest? How could one be sure that his horse came in last?

Suddenly Candidate A jumped onto the back of the spotted horse, which was to be his competitor's mount. He galloped to the end of the meadow and back on the spotted horse, thus ensuring that the animal he had been assigned, the brown horse, would finish last.

"Congratulations," the CEO said to him upon his return. "By illustrating innovative thinking, you have proven your worthiness to take over after I leave."

Candidate A succeeded by breaking through his habitual domain to think about winning in a completely different way.

The production department would produce only half a day, the other half they would work in sales.

The employees were excited to think that they might not have to lose their jobs and leave the company, but instead they could redesign the jobs they had to meet the challenge. They set to work with energy and will, and in three months, the company was again in the black, healthier even than before. And with improved morale.

Are people like Newton, Ford and Matsushita who see circumstances in different and productive ways extraordinarily talented or blessed? Or are they especially lucky? Not really.

Every person has unlimited potential. What we call talent (or blessings or luck) is usually some combination of determination and courage that helps a person stretch beyond even what he or she thinks is possible, into the realm of previously unimagined potential. Everyone can do this because everyone has a habitual domain and that domain can be expanded at will, with the right skills.

Using This Book

When we talk about your habitual domain we're talking about virtually everything you are. It's a vast, complex system of beliefs, information and practices, and it defies easy summation. When you first begin to envision your habitual domain, it may seem overwhelming. But improvement in your brain power is amazingly easy to achieve. And you don't need to do it all at once — you just need to approach it steadily.

Many studies in behavior show that a habit can be made or broken in two to three weeks of steady repetition. Learning to expand beyond habits can too.

Consider the work of Dr. Maxwell Maltz, a highly respected plastic surgeon who specializes in reconstructive surgery, especially in people who have been disfigured in fires or accidents. His ability to restore the original appearance of these victims is remarkable.

However, Maltz discovered that while the success of reconstructive surgery was often obvious as soon as the bandages were removed, the patient's self-image was slow to change. They had been living for some time inside scarred bodies and during that time, the burden of how they looked had created a whole set of attitudes and behaviors, from looking at the ground when talking to others to wearing only certain clothing to cover their deformities. After surgery, these patients retained the "I'm ugly" messages in their brains, despite assurances from everyone around them that their appearance had changed.

On the average Maltz found that it took about 21 days for his patients to feel better about themselves. It took three weeks to internalize the changes in their appearance and build new thought patterns.

To build new thought patterns about your own life, you could make a three-week plan to change your habitual domain. This book has 10 chapters. You could read a chapter a day for 10 days. Take the 11th day to map out your goals, based on your first reading. Then read the whole book again, more reflectively this time, a chapter a day. At the end of three weeks of reading and reflection you will find your thought patterns about yourself and your potential have changed. You will be well on your way to unleashing your unlimited potential.

You can approach the process more slowly. This is a way that has proven to be effective for many people who have studied habitual domains from my lecture notes and from texts and articles I have prepared previously.

Here's my advice:

First, read this book in its entirety. If you don't understand something the first time you encounter it, don't worry. Just move ahead. Don't let yourself bog down at a particular point, like "assessing your habitual domain." Soon, all the pieces will come together like a jigsaw puzzle.

In fact, you may want to read the book several times. Repetition and practice are vital to one's understanding of these concepts. The idea is to be so familiar with the ideas in this book that they become part of your mental software, where they can be effortlessly retrieved.

After you've read the book through at least once, you may find it works well for you to look at small pieces or concepts for

Any habit can be made or broken in about three weeks of steady effort. A simple exercise proves this. Choose a new place to keep your watch (or other item you usually wear every day). Every time you take it off for any reason, put it in that place. Within three weeks you will find yourself walking toward that place without thinking as soon as you reach to unfasten the watch.

more detailed consideration. Once a day, or more often, take a few minutes to open the book almost anywhere and absorb a few paragraphs. Read one of the illustrative anecdotes that explain the real-world application of these principles. Break the book down into the key concepts in an order that works best for you.

And don't just read passively. Get involved. For example, one chapter talks about the eight common behavior tendencies that you've unconsciously practiced all your life. Every morning pick a different tendency and be aware of how you use it during your day. You might want to keep a journal or use the worksheets in the back of the book.

When you find a practice or principle in this book that sounds right for you, put it to work immediately. Using it again and again will make it part of you. Before long it will do its work without your even consciously thinking about it.

The principles and ideas vital to the study of habitual domains are all interrelated. Like the many springs and gears of a wristwatch, they work in unison. You'll find that the same concept raised by one aspect of our study also pops up in several others. They form a interwoven tapestry. You will see some basic threads winding through the entire fabric of this book.

Here's another suggestion. When you discover something about yourself or others through the study of HDs, don't keep it to yourself. Share it with others — family members, friends, colleagues.

There's a very pragmatic reason for this. Just as the practice of any belief is strengthened and expanded by interaction with other believers, so your ideas and discoveries about habitual domains will be organized and strengthened by discussing them with others. The group is a powerful tool for learning and disciplining ourselves.

Indeed, HD clubs are popular among business professionals in Malaysia, China and my native Taiwan. By studying and discussing together the concepts of HD, the club members are able to expand their own habitual domains to include some of the knowledge and variations of behavior that are part of the habitual domains of others.

Most important to remember is this: Welcome challenges.

In your study of HD, I am confident that you will discover quickly how challenge stimulates growth. If we think in computer terms, handling a challenge requires updating or upgrading our software.

Welcome to the Journey

Gaining an understanding of your habitual domain and the habitual domain of others isn't an overnight effort. This book is only the beginning of a journey that will continue your entire life. Just as every journey starts with a single step, this book can be the guide you need to get started changing your life for the better, becoming the person you most want to be.

I can truthfully promise that understanding your habitual domain and learning to expand it will bring you riches. Not all of these riches will be monetary, although most people who work seriously at using the principles of habitual domain in their lives and careers will realize greater economic success. Indeed, the riches you reap will be the wealth of wisdom, for through your study of habitual domain you will understand some of the greatest mysteries of human life — the mysteries of the Self and the Self-With-Others.

Understanding of this kind is the wealth without which we face the worst kind of poverty, the poverty of ignorance and failure to fulfill ourselves. I sometimes say that by knowing HD you will never be poor, and without knowing HD you can never be rich.

As we begin, let me welcome you to this journey. And let me thank you for joining me. Through this book, we shall form a tie of friendship and shared goals.

P.L. Yu

您習慣領域的運作

Chapter 1

In the Realm of Your Habitual Domain

A simple exercise quickly illustrates the concept of habitual domain and the central theme of this book, which is the truth that you can change your capabilities by changing your mind. This exercise only takes a few seconds, but it will start you thinking about just how much you really can accomplish if you put your mind to it.

- Stand up and relax. Make a fist with your right hand and place it on top of your nose.
- Turn your body to the right without moving your legs. Memorize the farthest position to the right that your eyes can see.
- Return to your original standing position.
- In your mind, imagine returning to the starting position and turning again, only this time you will turn *two* times as far as you first did.
- Repeat the mental exercise, this time imagining that you've turned *three* times as far as you did initially.
- Now open your eyes, replace your fist to your nose, and actually turn to the right as far as possible.

You'll find that you've turned much farther than you did the first time.

This illustrates your mental power. It shows how easily you can increase the range of what you can accomplish if you put your mind to work.

This exercise is a metaphor for the expansion of your habitual domain. Although increasing your range of motion like this takes place in the physical world, it applies as well to our mental and spiritual selves.

The range of movement you exhibited in the first part of the exercise represents your **actual domain**, the parameters within which your body operates.

After visualizing a much larger range of movement — a **potential domain** — you found that your actual domain had enlarged, perhaps by as much as 15 to 25 percent.

In effect, you imagined a new domain for your body and it mobilized the physiological resources to create the flexibility needed to reach its new boundaries.

Why Our Habitual Domains Are Bounded

A similar thing happens with every human being and what might be described as the mind's range of movement. Each person has a unique set of behaviors resulting from his or her ways of thinking, judging, responding and handling problems. As we grow up, these factors gradually stabilize within a certain boundary. This collection of ways of thinking, coupled with its formation, interaction and dynamics, is called the **habitual domain**. On the simplest level, you could say that our habitual domain is where we "live," where we have our being, where our Self resides.

Our domains are formed for several reasons:

- The more we learn, the less the likelihood that an arriving event or piece of information is new to us.
- To interpret arriving events, we tend to relate them to past experiences.

- We tend to look for rhythms in our lives and force arriving events to conform to those rhythms.

As we gain experience, more of what happens to us seems familiar. We see this when we admire the wonder and innocent appreciation of children, who find so much that is new in every day. As we become adults, wonder is replaced with habit.

When we do encounter something new, we try to find a relationship between the new event and our stored memory. We use past experience to explain the new event. This is a basic brain response function, called ***analogy and association***.

Since we feel uncomfortable when we perceive an inconsistency between the event and our attitude or our behavior, we tend to explain a new event in a way that is consistent with attitudes and behaviors already in place. If they match up, we are comfortable again. In doing so, however, we actually may be distorting information, unwittingly seeing things as similar when in fact they are quite different.

As inhabitants of the natural world, we are most comfortable in a state of balance and harmony. When a new event comes our way, we try to fit it in to the rhythms in our lives that provide patterns or harmony.

This is only natural. The external world has natural rhythms, such as the changing of the seasons. Humans become aware of the rhythms of their environment and, becoming accustomed to them, tend to interpret new situations through familiar rhythms. For example, you might have observed that your relationships have a rhythm of infatuation, followed by boredom. Therefore, when you meet a new person, you may counsel yourself not to get too interested because you believe boredom will be close behind.

Because of the way our brains will normally handle arriving events, the new information that we learn diminishes daily. Unless extraordinary events occur, the knowledge we accumulate will be gradually bounded in a domain. We will proceed to learn less and less.

When you first go to work for a new company you will learn many things on your first day. On Day Two you will also be exposed to new ideas, but far fewer than on Day One. Before long, much of your job will be a routine and will become habitual.

Remember when you first began in a position you now hold. Were there tasks that were especially challenging then that you handle routinely and confidently now? How can you share this insight with people to make transitions in work or at home easier?

Reeds and Trees

A young sapling is green and flexible. When a strong wind forces it to bend, it usually whips back into shape.

Just so, a reed growing in a stream bends with the force of water and is not broken.

But as trees and reeds mature they become less and less flexible. They get stiff. Instead of bending with the wind and water, they offer resistance.

Their stiffness is a liability, for it allows a very strong wind or current to knock them over, break them or tear them from their roots.

Humans are no different. A flexible habitual domain allows you to bend, change, grow — to meet strong challenges without being broken by them. You're able to adapt to new ideas and overcome unexpected obstacles; you're always willing to absorb new information and ways of looking at the world.

Remain rigid, though, and a strong wind can blow you over.

Another way to think about this is to remember that living things are flexible in their growth phases but become stiffer as they near the end of life. Once stiffness sets in, they cannot withstand the pressures of weather and may break. Our brains are no different. If we remain open to experience, our brain is flexible and our knowledge can grow. If we let our set experiences become rigid, we will not be so able to withstand the pressures of life. The amount of new information you are exposed to will diminish every day. Soon, you will know all you think you need to know about your job. Your knowledge about the company soon will be bounded.

Who We Are, Not Who We Can Be

Forming a habitual domain is useful. It makes us more mature, skillful and efficient in dealing with routine problems. It gives us a base from which to operate in the world. In many ways, it is who we are.

But it has drawbacks. Though we may not be aware of it, our habitual domains limit our thoughts and make us predictable and uninventive. Our habitual domain is who we are, not who we can be.

Every habitual domain — whether it belongs to an individual, a small group of people, a company, a mass movement or even an entire nation — is unique. While different habitual domains may have many points in common, they will differ in specific details. For example, virtually every corporation has as part of its habitual domain a faith in the free enterprise system, but the ways in which companies pursue profits vary hugely.

Because of their different habitual domains, individuals will interpret situations and come up with solutions in very different ways. This marvelous capacity illustrates the uniqueness of each person and the unlimited potential each of us has to become what we want to be.

Because the habitual domains of individuals are so varied and so potentially powerful, a successful leader must have a habitual domain large enough to understand and judge the different thinking and reactions coming from the habitual domains of the people he or she encounters. In effect, their habitual domains must be made part of the leader's habitual domain if the group (an organization of any size or kind, even a country) is to be genuinely productive.

Likewise, to relate successfully to other people, an individual must be able to take the habitual domains of others into account. Sometimes we hear the phrase "make room for" when people are talking about each other. A woman might say, "My neighbor was cranky this morning because our dog had torn open her garbage bags, but I made room for her being mad. I know her mother is coming to visit today and she is especially anxious for her home to look clean."

This act of "making room for" another's feelings or ideas is really a good visual description of expanding your own habitual domain to take in someone else's habits of thinking, to understand them better.

When we know why we have habitual domains and what they mean to our behaviors, we can see more clearly what drives our own actions as well as what causes others to behave as they do. Napoleon's rise and fall illustrates how others' habitual domains can work for or against us depending on our awareness of them.

Napoleon's Rise and Fall

Napoleon Bonaparte's success in establishing an empire can largely be attributed to his brilliant military strategies, with which he was familiar and comfortable but which were outside the comprehension of his enemies' habitual domains.

A prime example was Napoleon's march over the Alps to attack Austria. Conventional wisdom at the time was that the Alps posed an insurmountable natural obstacle that no army could overcome. Napoleon, however, anticipated the problems his army would encounter and was ready when they surfaced. His French troops did march across the mountains and caught the Austrian troops out of position.

The Austrians finally realized what was going on and tried to adjust by getting ready for attack — in other words, they tried to expand and adjust their HDs to deal with this threat — but it was too late. Napoleon crushed their armies.

Napoleon's habitual domain was bigger than that of his enemies. He developed strategies that were unknown and unpredictable to them.

Ironically, Napoleon eventually was defeated because in time his own HD became static and predictable while those of opposing generals became more flexible and expansive. Napoleon then found himself in the position of the Austrians — confronted with an enemy whose strategies he could not predict or understand.

The Duke of Wellington employed a brilliant strategy for waging guerrilla war against the French occupation forces in Spain. His army of English and Spanish troops vanished when the French arrived and emerged when the French retreated. Direct confrontations with the French were limited, but Wellington's hit-and-run tactics weakened the French army and even eroded the French economy.

On the Russian front, Marshal Kutuzov dealt with Napoleon's invading army by retreating, destroying all shelter and supplies that might fall into French hands. This destruction of Russian property by Russians flabbergasted the French; it was unprecedented in "civilized" warfare. But it was a highly effective strategy. The advancing Napoleonic army was denied food and shelter. Supply lines back to France were long and slow-moving.

When the French finally took Moscow they found much of it burning. National churches had been torched by the Russians lest they be desecrated or occupied by the French. The invaders simply could not believe this behavior.

With the arrival of winter, Kutuzov's strategy became clear. The French army had been drawn deep into enemy territory with brutal weather on the way. Its supply lines were vulnerable and unreliable.

Napoleon ordered a retreat, but it was too late.

His freezing, starving men stumbled back to France, all the while being harassed by Kutuzov's army, which now was on the offensive.

Napoleon's fall was, in large part, the result of his pride. Because of his early innovations and repeated victories, he came to think of himself as unbeatable. He felt so secure with the superiority of his own habitual domain that he saw no reason to study the habitual domains of his opponents. This was a fatal mistake.

Individual behavior and strategy is tremendously influenced by our habitual domains. The rise and fall of an entire country or empire can be determined by the growth or stabilization of a leader's habitual domain.

Charting the Boundaries of Your Habitual Domain

Habitual domains are created by the interaction of four elements within our minds: goals, state evaluation, charges and attention allocation. Once we begin to understand the basics of how our minds — and these four elements — work, it's easy to alter or expand our habitual domains.

Goals and State Evaluation

Goal setting is one of the major tools we use in expanding our habitual domains. **Goals** are a fundamental part of our behavior function. Even the most unambitious person has goals, though he or she may not consciously be aware of them. Using the human urge to reach goals is natural and easy, once we begin to see the basics of how our brains work.

Some of our goals have been pre-programmed into our brains by millennia of evolution: individual survival, for instance, or perpetuation of the species.

Other goals have been acquired through our life experiences: the accumulation of wealth, the desire for prestige or fame, even the compulsion to perform good deeds.

As a parallel to goal setting, we also continuously evaluate where we are relative to the goals. This function is called **state evaluation**.

Simply by beginning a study of habitual domains, you are improving your competitive abilities.

Consider how many basketball games are won by just a point or two. Those two points may not seem like much, but they provided the margin of victory. Sometimes just a little bit of effort can make all the difference.

Every day that you spend some time working on your habitual domain sharpens your competitive edge. An understanding of habitual domains gives you an advantage. This is the margin of excellence that puts you ahead.

When all of these goals — and there can be thousands within an individual — are reached or held in equilibrium, we feel content. But when we fall short of those goals, when our perceived situations don't live up to our ideals, we become frustrated or uneasy.

This is easy to explain at a physical level. If, for example, your heart or kidneys are healthy you will pay little attention to them. Their goal of functioning effectively is being realized. But if you find yourself continuously paying attention to these organs, whether because of pain or simply because something "just doesn't feel right," there's a good chance you have a physical problem.

Similarly, if a company's sales are in good shape, its employees probably aren't going to spend much time worrying about sales. If, on the other hand, much time is devoted daily to thinking of ways to improve sales, it's a sign that the sales department is ineffective.

A person who is in a challenging position may be working hard but may find his skills are in equilibrium with the challenges the job presents. If the job is way too easy, he will likely feel unfulfilled, even bored.

Charges and Attention Allocation

This feeling of a goal being unmet, of a lack of equilibrium within an individual (or an organization), leads to an emotional jolt. I refer to it as a **charge** because this heightened feeling is actually caused by neurons in your brain "lighting up," or becoming activated by a stimulating event.

Charges can be created within us by many different things. A failure in business, your children performing poorly in school, financial problems, attacks on your reputation, illness, overwork — these are just a few of the obvious situations in which charges may be created. Charges can also be more elementary: Hunger, fatigue and fear all result in charges.

A charge can be dramatic — you hear a train whistle and see an oncoming beam of light as you are crossing the railroad track. A charge can also be very subtle.

For example, how much attention do you pay each day to

A favorable state evaluation leads to feelings of increased competence and ability. Your positive attitude reflects in your work and relationships with others. Self-suggestion, pep talks and faith talks are used by successful individuals every day for motivation. How often do you evaluate your state? What are good times to do this? Everyone has a special time of day when the forces of self-suggestion are most powerful. When is your time?

A charge is the emotional jolt you feel when there is a gap between one of your goals and the reality in your life.

your heart? An hour? Twenty minutes? Ten minutes? Even five?

Chances are you pay absolutely no attention to your heart, other than providing the routine maintenance of exercise and a healthy diet. And that's as it should be. A healthy, properly maintained heart will go about its job effectively and unobtrusively. When your heart is operating well, your cardiovascular system is usually in equilibrium.

But if you find yourself continuously paying attention to your heart because in some way it attracts your attention — perhaps it races, or beats heavily, or seems to skip in its rhythm— there's a good chance that something is out of balance. It may be time to see a doctor.

Your feelings of uneasiness regarding your heart are a charge, a charge that has been created because something isn't right. Your body is telling you something important. When all is in harmony, no charge is created and your attention is not drawn to your heart, or any other singular part of your body.

But do not think that charges are necessarily negative in meaning. The gap between a goal and reality can as easily be an opportunity as a shortcoming. For example, you may attend a seminar in which the speaker deeply impresses and moves you, filling you with hope, energy and determination. This, too, is a charge.

Charges don't come one at a time. They arrive from many directions and change rapidly. The brain pays attention to whichever situation seems to have the most significance within the overall *charge structure* — that is, the totality of the charges that individuals carry and the effects created by the charges.

For example, you may have worried all morning that you are performing poorly at your job. This worry creates an overwhelming charge that will hardly let you think about anything else.

If over the lunch hour, though, you find yourself facing an armed mugger on the street, your charge structure will abruptly shift. Suddenly job problems seem insignificant; far more important is the need to survive this dangerous situation. Your mind instantly practices *attention allocation*. It decides what is most worthy of your attention — in this case, survival.

Steadily throughout your waking hours, your mind

Think about the most successful people you know. How do you describe their success? Is there a difference in the way they allocate their attention and the way not so successful people do?

11

assesses the charges created by everything that affects you, from the scratchy label on your shirt collar to your religious beliefs. Attention allocation can be a reaction to something that presents itself — like the mugger mentioned earlier — or it can be directed. Purposefully allocating attention is the way we make changes.

Overwork and exhaustion can create charges as well. When our energy is significantly depleted, the charge level can be very high. At that point the brain tells the body to rest. After sleeping (or, perhaps, spending a few moments in meditation or relaxation exercises), you will find that the charge level will be lowered significantly. At that point your attention can be focused on whatever are the most important remaining influences on your charge structure.

Releasing Charges

How do you get rid of or reduce a charge that is making you uncomfortable, leaving you feeling unfulfilled or provoking you to action? Basically we have two ways of **releasing charges**.

The first is **active problem solving**. A goal is not being reached; therefore you start looking for ways to reach the goal. If your goal is to earn more money, you begin examining the possibilities for additional income: overtime, freelance work, part-time jobs, a new investment strategy, earning a promotion.

With this method, the charge can be transformed into **drive** to help us achieve our goals.

The second option is **avoidance justification**. This means we readjust our ideal goals. We may try to rationalize situations to lower the need for high goals, making our current state more acceptable.

You may tell yourself that the accumulation of wealth brings with it problems of its own, problems you are not prepared to deal with. You lower your goal of earning more.

To release charges we tend to select the action which leads to the lowest remaining charge. The remaining charge is the resistance to total discharge. This is called the **least resistance** principle.

Active problem solving can transform a charge into drive to get the job or goal achieved, while avoidance justification lets the charge leak out, without finishing the job, in order to restore a peaceful state of mind. In what situations have you used avoidance justification instead of active problem solving? How can you reverse your desire to do this?

A charge can lead to drive and to achieving goals.

13

Have you noticed when you have something steadily on your mind (anything from a vacation destination to an illness), it suddenly seems you hear about it more than ever before? Facing a non-routine problem, we need information to supplement our competence in the decision process. How does attention allocation sensitize us to information (solicited or unsolicited) that we would normally screen out?

Perhaps you realize that your desire for more money cannot be reached without a tremendous sacrifice of your family life. You decide the need to spend time with your loved ones is greater than your need for more money. According to the least resistance principle, you will opt for the course of action that will result in the least overall charge or frustration. (On the other hand, your family members may complain so loudly about lack of money that you decide taking a second job is the course of least resistance.)

Avoidance justification can be very valuable because frequently we establish inappropriate or unrealistic goals for ourselves. For example, we may be strongly motivated by a desire for revenge against someone we believe has wronged us. This is an unworthy goal, one that needs to be readjusted for our own good. When a goal is shown to be unworthy or unwise, we can shift our attention to another goal and initiate a more productive process in our brains and behavior.

Goals, state evaluation, charges and attention allocation determine, to a large extent, our habitual domains. In upcoming chapters, you will learn how to define and evaluate your goals so you will increase your awareness of the circumstances that create a charge in you and gain a better understanding of your personal charge structure. And you will be able to alter your own ways of thinking so that you enlarge your habitual domain and meet your goals for prosperity, well-being and other elements of your own special definition of happiness.

The Delusional Messiah

Our thoughts and behaviors are closely linked to the activities of our neural cells, the activated circuit patterns. Our thoughts and behaviors — even attitudes and feelings — change as the circuit patterns change.

Indeed, we are happy because happy circuit patterns occupy our attention. The same is true for feelings of anger or sadness. As circuit patterns, just like computer programs, can be changed or controlled, so can our emotions and states of mind.

The story of the "delusional messiah" illustrates this dramatically. Once a man believed himself to be Jesus Christ, and conventional psychotherapy and drugs seemed to make no difference. He clung to his delusion and continued proclaiming himself the Messiah.

Finally, one psychiatrist came up with a daring method of treatment.

The physician approached the patient with a measuring tape and said, "Jesus, I need to find out how tall you are." He then measured the man's height.

"Now spread out your arms. I want to measure from hand to hand," the doctor said.

Later the doctor had two large pieces of lumber brought in and proceeded to have them cut to his specifications.

The patient asked about the wood.

"Well," said the psychiatrist, "if you're going to convince people that you're Jesus, you're going to have to be crucified. I'm having your cross built right now."

The patient turned pale and announced that he really wasn't Jesus at all. From that moment on, his delusions vanished. The doctor's presentation changed dramatically the patient's goal, state evaluation and attention allocation.

In habitual domain terms, what happened there was that the announcement that he was going to be crucified created a tremendous surge of charge in the patient's mind. With such a high level of charge, the brain quickly tries to find a way to release it.

Usually the release comes in the form of a decision, an action or a change in behavior. In the case of the delusional patient, his mind quickly recognized that the easiest way to avoid crucifixion was to drop his claims of divinity.

Consider some of the problems you have experienced lately. How was the situation at the time of the problem different from an ideal situation? In your effort to bring your situation to equilibrium, did you use active problem solving or avoidance justification? How would the outcome have been different if you had used the opposite method to reduce your charge?

實現您無限的潛能

16

Chapter 2
Realizing Your Unlimited Potential

What keeps us from meeting our goals? Perhaps an even more important question is: What keeps us from realizing our unlimited potential, from reaching goals we don't even dare to set?

Many people settle for far less in life than they should. Their potential brain power so far outdistances the image they have of their own capabilities that they cannot even imagine what they can truly accomplish.

Anyone who has been a teacher knows that the most important part of teaching is not sharing information. It is helping students discover their capacity to learn. Once students discover this, they are not limited to just the information their teacher can share — all information is theirs for the taking.

If you have been present at the moment that a baby first walks, you have seen the magical moment when a person really feels the promise of his or her own potential. With the first successful steps, the baby shows to the world a facial expression shining with wonder ("Can I really do this?") and power ("Yes! I am doing this!").

And, of course, joy. What a joy it is to discover our personal potential.

Why People Don't Realize Their Potential

Yet if the process is so full of wonder, power and joy, why does it seem mysterious and difficult? Why are more people not realizing their potential?

The basic reasons are two. First, by the time we have reached adolescence, our habitual domain has been built by our childhood experiences and learning, by our environment, by our heredity and by all the other elements that go to make up the way we think.

Second, most people don't know much about the way the human brain is "programmed." They understand some fundamentals about how to add to their knowledge base — read, get information from other people, travel and observe — but they don't know much about how the brain uses that knowledge. And they don't know how to change patterns already in place in the brain.

They become accustomed to living inside the habitual domain they have already built. It's comfortable enough, in most cases. Furthermore, most people simply never realize that they have a habitual domain and that they can change its boundaries and enlarge it at will.

Alinsky's Experiment

A very telling example of how much most people stay within their own habitual domains is the story of social activist Saul Alinsky's experiment in downtown Los Angeles, trying to give away a $10 bill. Without offering any explanation, he stood on a street corner, holding out a $10 bill to the first five people who passed him. Not one took the money. They said,

"I have no change with me."

"I have no money on me."

"I'm not that kind of girl."

"I don't come that cheap."

"What kind of con game is this? If you don't go away, I will call the police."

In every case, the habitual domain of the passerby did not

include the idea that a man on a street corner might simply give away $10, no strings attached.

If any one of them could have let this new idea into the habitual domain, he or she would have been $10 richer in an instant.

When we have become adults and our habitual domains are pretty comprehensive — they cover most of our lives and go with us the way a turtle shell covers the turtle — expanding our habitual domains simply doesn't occur to most of us. The phrase in English that a person has "made up his mind" is very interesting to me as I think about habitual domains and the way the brain works. In a very real way, each of us has "made" up his mind, has built a way of thinking, literally, by establishing patterns in the brain.

These are called "circuit patterns," and learning about them is the key to changing your habitual domain at will.

Understanding and Changing Circuit Patterns

Our thoughts, concepts and ideas are represented by different **circuit patterns** in the brain. Just as the circuitry in a piece of electronic equipment is designed to perform a specific function within the device, so the circuit patterns in our brains allow us to retrieve and employ certain concepts, ideas or activities.

These circuit patterns are reinforced when the corresponding ideas are repeatedly used or rehearsed.

For example, let's say you are working on an assembly line screwing a certain nut onto a certain bolt as the product moves past you. Initially you will move slowly and hesitantly. You may drop the nut or your tools. You may strip the threads through incorrect placement of the nut. And you may only fulfill this task 25 times an hour while your more experienced co-workers do it 50 times an hour.

Circuit patterns are the actual templates of neural cells that are activated for every thought, idea or memory we have. These patterns can be created spontaneously and we can also program them purposely.

Athletes know what rehearsal and practice mean to a sport.

But over time your mind/body coordination improves. Before long you are doing the work naturally and almost without effort. You have established a circuit pattern for that particular activity, and it only becomes stronger with additional use.

We establish a new circuit pattern in our brain when we learn a new theory, fact or behavior. It's much like introducing a new program or piece of data into a computer.

Rehearsal and Practice

Rehearsal and practice are important in strengthening our circuit patterns. For Americans, the characters that make up the Chinese language are complex and incomprehensible. Yet the Chinese, because they have practiced them repeatedly since childhood, have established strong circuit patterns in their brains that make it easy for them to write and read these characters.

Penfield's Experiment

Circuit patterns can be physically observed. Wilder Penfield, a famous Canadian physician who specialized in brain surgery as a cure for epilepsy, made an intriguing discovery during one of his operations.

Before surgery, the doctor used a small electrode to touch parts of the patient's brain to determine whether they were affected by the irregular electrical discharges that characterize epileptic seizures.

On one occasion he touched the neurons at a patient's temple and triggered a particular memory. Remarkably, whenever the same amount of voltage was applied to the same part of the brain, the patient would vividly recall the same memory from his childhood. It was an incredibly detailed account of his playing with another child, a series of images containing information that the patient normally couldn't remember.

The incident proved that every memory is stored somewhere in our brains (in the potential domain) as patterns of neurons, or brain cues. As long as the neurons that form the circuit pattern for that memory remain alive, we can retrieve the information with the appropriate stimulus.

Circuit patterns can be built or made stronger by repetition. When you practice or rehearse a thought process (or a skill like playing the piano, or a physical activity like jumping rope, for that matter), the corresponding circuit pattern becomes stronger.

Have you learned to type? If so, you know that repetition and practice are essential. You have to practice every day to master typing.

In fact, even when you're not at the keyboard you may find yourself mentally typing, breaking down words into letters and, in your mind, using the appropriate finger to tap the appropriate typewriter key.

In the process you are establishing stronger circuit patterns.

As a boy in Taiwan I learned to perform mathematical computations on an abacus. I practiced daily, and after a while I was able to do computations in my head, simply by imagining an abacus in my mind.

When was the last time you had a totally new idea? What was the idea? What triggered you to have the idea?

Ideas and the Operators That Change Them

Information, or an arriving event, is programmed in our brains in circuit patterns. Neurologists who have experimented with primates show us that these patterns are as observable as lighted circuitry on electronic devices. Neurons activate or "light up" in some chartable patterns, patterns that are seemingly identical every time the behavior is repeated, the thought is thought, or the memory is recalled.

We possess two essential kinds of circuit patterns. These are **ideas** and **operators**.

Ideas are essentially static, or set in a lasting pattern. For example, it's unlikely that a person's memories of a peak event, say a wedding day, are going to change. They are more or less fixed.

Or consider numbers. One is always one, two is always two. They're not going to change.

Why Bother?

Why make the commitment to understand and expand your own HD? Will it make you rich? Happy? Wise? Successful? Yes, it can.

If you're determined to earn your first million by a certain age or to become president of your company, working on your habitual domain will help get you there — or as close as you personally can be. Understanding the power of habitual domains can help you achieve any goal you set.

But more importantly, being aware of your HD will provide something enormously valuable — and more difficult to gain than wealth for many people: a sense of balance in your life.

We've all heard stories of business and professional people, entertainers and others who fought furiously to reach a particular goal, but once they had achieved it found they were somehow dissatisfied. For all their accomplishments, they felt oddly incomplete.

A person who truly understands his or her HD will certainly be capable of achieving fame, fortune and power. If those are the goals you set for yourself, knowing your HD will be part of your success in reaching them.

But you will also maintain a balance, a sense of stability (financially, emotionally, spiritually) that will see you through almost anything.

This is not to say that if you diligently develop your HD, no harm ever will befall you. Reversals and losses — both in business and in life — are everyone's fate.

But for the earnest HD practitioner, reversals and other temporary setbacks will be offset by the deeply satisfying pleasures and accomplishments that accompany a healthy, flexible, growing habitual domain.

An ***operator*** is a different sort of circuit pattern which allows us to change and reorder these static ideas into new relationships which create new ideas.

For example, simple addition is an arithmetic operator which allows us to deal with unchanging numbers in a new way. Thus, if we combine one and two we get three.

An egg and a rock are two different things. The idea of the egg or the rock — what we know it looks like, where we know it comes from, what we know it is made of — is essentially fixed. But if we compare them, the act of comparison is an operator: An egg is a living thing, a rock is not; both can be thrown; one will break and one will not. These are new ideas resulting from the comparison of static ideas.

In the abstract, our habitual domain is the collection of all the ideas and operators that exist as circuit patterns in our brains. Some of these ideas and operators have very strong circuit patterns. Others are relatively weak.

When we're called upon to process new information, to analyze incoming events or to make judgments, it's the strongest ideas and operators — the ones of which we are most conscious — that we'll draw upon first.

Because we all have different habitual domains, we may react differently to the same object, image or event. The way we interpret and judge arriving events depends on the degree of attention we give to how and what combinations of ideas and operators are activated.

We can understand ourselves better when we become aware of how ideas and operators work in our minds. We can change behavior, knowledge, even belief, when we purposefully activate an operator to deal with a static idea we already have.

Pavlov's Dogs

The Russian scientist Pavlov is responsible for one of the world's most famous experiments. Though his subjects were dogs, the results apply to humans as well.

In the experiment, dogs were fed a piece of meat shortly after the ringing of a bell. The meat and the ringing of the bell were associated with happy events to the dog, which also built a circuit pattern connecting the ringing with the meat and with the happiness of eating. After several repeti-

One use of the word "paradigm" can mean a circuit pattern for a self-imposed limitation we have developed over time and placed on ourselves, sometimes at an unconscious level. A paradigm can take many forms, from the belief that you cannot sing or draw, or are not good at math, or are not outgoing, to the feeling that you can't succeed in life. Any limit you impose on yourself can be considered a paradigm; believing it results in self-fulfilling outcomes. Think about the paradigms you have imposed on yourself and what you can do to stop believing them.

tions, the dogs started to salivate at the sound of the bell even though no meat was given them. The dogs had learned to associate the ringing of a bell with meat even without the presence of meat because the corresponding circuit patterns were strong enough.

The experiment was further refined. A dog was conditioned to salivate only when a high-frequency bell was rung. Then, when a low-frequency bell was rung, an electric shock was administered to the animal.

The shocks frightened the dog; before long, the dog began to shake whenever it heard the low-frequency bell. It wasn't necessary even to administer the electric shock — at the sound of the low-frequency bell, the animal acted as if it were being shocked.

Then the frequencies of the two bells were modified so that their sounds became more and more similar. When the frequencies were so close that the dog could not distinguish between them, and the animal couldn't be sure whether it was going to receive food or a shock, it developed neurotic behavior. This could be due to confusion in the activation of proper circuit patterns.

When the frequencies of the bells were readjusted to increase their differences, the dog's behavior returned to normal. Based on the sounds, it once again knew whether to expect food or a shock.

When confronted with a new event, the brain first investigates its features and attributes to establish a relationship — an analogy or an association of the new event to the already known. The whole of one's past knowledge is brought to bear in understanding the new event.

When we change a circuit pattern, the change becomes part of our habitual domain and is applied to all the new events and information we encounter. That's why even small changes can matter a great deal to improving our lives.

Just as a computer runs on software or programming, so the human brain has its own programming. These are thoughts, concepts and ideas that form circuit patterns. Even though we may not be consciously aware of them, these patterns often dictate how we react to certain situations and stimuli.

Circuit patterns are always changing as new data is introduced to our mental computers, but they remain powerful forces inside each of us. Consider, for example, the common emotion of anger. When anger takes over, it can result in physiological changes — a reddened face, sweating, increased heartbeat. That's the work of the anger circuit pattern established in our brains over an entire lifetime.

You can turn off that circuit and get rid of the anger.

Try smiling. It sounds too simple to be effective, but the next time you are angry, force yourself to smile.

Circuit patterns already in your brain link smiling with happy thoughts. When you smile, 40 or so facial muscles send a "happy" message to your brain.

At that point the brain shifts into its happy circuit patterns. Next time you feel your anger rising, try smiling or laughing. You won't be able to become angry, or at least not to the degree you would otherwise. You'll have learned an important lesson about controlling your emotions and about your ability to repattern your brain at will.

The Elephant's Limitation

Under a circus bigtop you may find huge elephants tethered with slender ropes to the poles that hold up the tent. These powerful animals could easily break the rope or pull down the pole — but they don't even try to escape. It's because they are prisoners of their limited habitual domains.

When these mighty creatures were small, their trainers tied them to strong concrete or steel columns with an unbreakable metal chain. Initially, the young elephants struggled to escape, but their efforts were in vain. After a few months, they became used to their situation. They acquired a habit, or a program, if you think of the elephant's brain as a computer.

Now, whenever these elephants find themselves roped to a column their programming tells them — and they believe — that there is no way to escape. So they never try.

To realize your true potential, beware of habits that restrict your thinking and actions. Instead, build circuit patterns for flexibility, adventure and freedom. Welcome new ideas.

發現您習慣領域的核心

Chapter 3

Discovering the Core of Your Habitual Domain

e know that each of us has a habitual domain. But our brain is not limited to this. In fact, the very lack of limits is what makes understanding our habitual domain exciting.

The anatomy of our habitual domain is made up of these elements:

- **Potential Domain**: This is the collection of all the ideas and operators that can potentially be activated in our brain.
- **Actual Domain**: The ideas and operators that actually are being used at one time. The tossing of two coins can be metaphor for this. There are four possible outcomes of heads and tails (the potential domain), but only one actual outcome (actual domain). Thus the actual domain is the only domain that occupies our attention at a given moment. It's our mental focus point.
- **Activation Probability**: The probability that particular ideas and operators will be activated.
- **Reachable Domain**: When we activate a set of ideas and operators, we can generate new sets of ideas and operators. These new ideas and operators are the reachable domain.

In every person the potential domain is enormous. Every sound, every sight, every meeting, every book — indeed, every experience — can become part of a person's domain.

In fact, however, a person accesses a very small part of this potential universe of knowledge, feeling and action. The part that is being accessed is the actual domain. Many things diminish our ability to reach the potential within ourselves. Factors ranging from health, to opportunity, to self-imposed failures can restrict us and affect the probability that we will activate even a small portion of the potential available in our brains. Our reachable domain is how much we can and will activate. The point of understanding our habitual domain is the ability to pull more "potential" into our actual domain, to be able to use more of what is really available in our virtually limitless power.

The drive to tap this power is as individual as the power itself. Some people will reach more of their potential than others because they focus more intently upon the possibilities.

The Glass Salesman

Some years ago, Corning Glass developed a shatterproof glass product. At the annual event to recognize sales performance, one salesman's achievements were so far beyond the rest that he was asked to share with the entire sales force the secret of his success. He explained that he simply put a piece of the shatter-proof glass in front of a potential customer and struck it as hard as he could with a hammer. Everyone who saw the demonstration placed an order.

The company was so excited about the technique that it ordered kits with a hammer and pieces of glass made for every salesman. The next year, the same man was again salesperson of the year. The rest of the sales force wondered why, when they all had the same tools, he had again beaten all their efforts. He explained that he hadn't used the kit. Once it had become "standard issue" for the sales force, the hammer and glass example was no longer fresh for him, he said. Instead, he had found another way to demonstrate to customers the qualities of the glass he was selling by letting his customers hit the glass themselves.

This story illustrates several crucial elements of using an

Some people will reach more of their potential than others because they will focus more intently on the possibilities.

Do you have unlimited potential? What is the greatest thing you could accomplish in your lifetime if from now on everything went just as you would want it to? What is the greatest thing you would like to accomplish if things go as they have been in your life? What is the greatest thing you really expect to accomplish? Are these answers different? Why?

28

awareness of habitual domain to release our personal best efforts. First, the successful salesman looked at the possibilities of his task in a new way and struck upon the hammer and glass demonstration. No doubt his presentation was appealing not only because of the physical example of the shatter-proof glass but because of the energy the man brought to striking the glass with the hammer. That kind of energy kept him from staying with the method the following year. When the hammer and glass kit became part of his habitual domain, he reached again to his potential domain and found another approach. This let him beat the performance of the sales people who were satisfied with the kit they were handed and looked no further.

To be able to tap our unlimited power and potential, we first need to locate our own special habitual domain. Every person "lives" or has the center of his or her being in a different "place." That place is our habitual domain. To grow we have to expand its boundaries. We do that by understanding how our minds work.

Habitual domain is the collection of ideas and operators existing in our minds. These ideas and operators make us who we are. That is why different people treat the same experience differently. We activate different ideas and operators when we deal with different events or problems.

The Core of Your Habitual Domain

The probability of a certain idea or operator being activated will vary depending upon many factors — everything that bears upon us at a certain moment. Those ideas and operators that have the highest probability of being activated are the **core** of the habitual domain.

The habitual domain's core contains your strongest beliefs, ideas and operators, represented by very strong circuit patterns, many of them learned from your parents or other role models when you are young. They become strong

Your habitual domain is the collection of ideas and operators existing in your mind — it is unique. No one else will experience life in exactly the same way you will.

ideas and operators through repetition over time. Unless you are forced to change them (as recruits in military boot camp who are made to fold socks in a highly particular way will fold them that way the rest of their lives), or are confronted by another culture (as immigrants are), or have some reason to examine your core thoughts carefully, they will dictate your behavior without your even being aware of it.

In psychology, mental processes that occur without conscious awareness are called the subconscious. The subconscious may be regarded as part of the collection of ideas and operators that make up your potential domain. They may not catch your attention at the moment (that is, they aren't in your actual domain), but under proper conditions — say, when you're in a quiet environment or when your charge structure is at a very low level — they will come to your attention and affect your behaviors and thoughts.

Ideas and operators are very strong, but they are not set in stone. While certain ideas are at the core of the way you look at the world, even the ideas that make up your subconscious can be changed.

But to do so, you must be aware of and work with eight common behavior tendencies, extremely strong circuit patterns that can be activated quickly and without much conscious effort to process information and affect your behavior.

Think of times when you said to yourself you were too scared, too nervous, too unsure to do something you very much wanted to do. Analyze what it was that you felt was lacking. Very likely the fear was a result of your habitual domain. Realizing what limited you from growing is the first step in allowing yourself to grow. Make a list of three such situations and as the opportunities present themselves again, address the issues that held you back and do whatever it was you once passed up.

Eight Strong Behavior Patterns

Activating these behavior tendencies can be very useful as shortcuts in assessing others and your relationships with them. But they have pitfalls as well, and you must always be alert when employing them.

When you read these, you may say, "Of course. These behaviors are so obvious." They are common, indeed, but that is why they are worth examining. These tendencies are so strongly a part of our unconscious behavior that we may not recognize them in ourselves — sometimes with negative results. We are used to seeing ourselves in a broad view, not to examining specifics. We look at the forest, not the trees.

All these behaviors affect our relations with others.

Behavior and beliefs learned in childhood make up a big part of the core of a person's habitual domain.

Compare similarities and differences between your boss or a senior colleague and you. How do these similarities or differences affect your working relationships?

Much of our potential domain — our chance to change and grow — comes from our interaction with other people. It is important to keep an "open mind" in the best sense — to let the boundaries of our personal habitual domain be open to visitors, people from whom we can learn.

SOCIAL COMPARISON

To reach our desired goals, we need to understand our state and position in society — in our close relationships, our neighborhoods, our workplaces. If we don't have objective information or standards by which to make such an evaluation, we will make it by comparing ourselves with people whom we think are in the same social circumstances as we are.

Social comparison is a vital tool for individual survival. A very obvious example is represented by the familiar saying, "When in Rome, do as the Romans do." In other words, when you're in an unfamiliar place, you observe the behavior of others and pattern your actions after theirs. Your odds of getting along in that particular environment are then improved.

Clearly, in a business environment, comparison can be crucial to success. A new employee who cannot fit into a corporate culture probably won't last in the company. And the global marketplace demands that business people use social comparison to avoid being insensitive to the social customs of colleagues or clients from cultures other than their own.

The social comparison method is a fast and simple way to expand your habitual domain, but you must be aware of the following points:

- To work, the background conditions must be similar and comparable. There's no point in comparing an adult to an infant. But comparing common behaviors of adults does provide meaningful and useful results.
- The comparison must have a focus. You cannot assume that because a person is good at mathematics, he or she will be good at other subjects. A teacher who picks a class leader on the basis of that person's grades may find that grades are no indication of leadership ability.

Focus on the precise qualities you want to examine in your comparison. Be specific.

- Practice modesty and be aware of others' feelings.

When making comparisons, be alert to the possibility that you may react to the process in negative ways.

If you conclude that you are stronger, more successful or superior to the person you are comparing yourself to, the result could be pride and self-satisfaction. That reaction can be destructive enough even if you keep it to yourself. If you make it obvious to others, you could find yourself being rejected or isolated. Nobody likes a snob.

It is best, under such circumstances, to practice humility and caution in your dealings with others.

If, on the other hand, you determine from your comparison that others are superior to you, you might react with jealousy and resentment. You could become bitter, and you might abandon your efforts at self-improvement as useless.

A more positive reaction to finding yourself in an inferior position would be to learn from others, increasing your confidence and skills. At the same time, you mark yourself as an individual willing to work hard to improve yourself. And, by asking others to teach you, you pay them a high compliment which will only increase their willingness to help you out.

Social comparisons are extensively utilized in management. A company may publicize the efforts of each division and reward the division with the best performance. This can create incentive and increase productivity. Another tactical use of social comparison is to put "successful" people in the spotlight to create a standard for achievement. Thus naming an employee of the month can increase the charge and drive in others to perform and compete.

For an individual trying to reach a goal, comparison to an admired person, a role model, can be helpful as an example and incentive. It is not necessary to be in personal contact with the role model. Even reading a biography of a person who has the character or achievements you admire can have a positive effect on your habitual domain.

HALO EFFECT

When judging others, we tend to classify subjects into two groups, good or bad. People who seem to be "good" take on all the positive

In your office or in another group you are part of, look around at the people you are with. Have you already subconsciously classified them? Are there some people you prefer to work near? Why? Can you state what it is about each person that attracts you or turns you off? Do these people know you have classified them? Is classifying a good habit in some situations? Will changing your classifications be positive for the working environment?

attributes of good people; people who seem to be "bad" take on all the negative attributes of bad people.

This is an ancient response, meant for protection.

When you meet someone for the first time, do you try to quickly categorize them as a friend or as an enemy? Perhaps as "my kind of person" or "not my kind of person"? Most people do. It's why "success coaches" warn business people that they have only a couple of minutes to make a lasting favorable impression on an interviewer or a potential client.

The trouble, of course, is that incomplete knowledge can be misleading. An unwashed person in ragged clothing may be quickly identified as uneducated, incompetent and unreliable. Of course, none of those things is necessarily true. An attractive individual in good clothes may seem smart, intelligent, capable and reliable, but could as easily be a con artist.

The halo effect is one of our standard evaluation methods from childhood on. When called upon to process a large amount of information (say, at a party attended by many strangers) we speed up and simplify the process by categorizing the people who are there in two classes.

Based on their clothing, body language and other external indicators, we decide that a person is good or bad and attribute to them good or bad characteristics. It's a simple process and, for most people, past experience has usually shown it to be very useful.

The problem is, the halo effect can cause errors in judgment if not used with the proper caution. It's the same dilemma as when we use a point to represent an area. We know only a little, but we generalize a lot. And oversimplification leads to mistakes.

You must always keep in mind that at first meeting you have seen only a small portion of another individual. What's more, people change over time. The behavior on which you judge that person may not even be typical of him, or he may abandon that sort of behavior in the future.

The best advice is to avoid quick judgments.

PROJECTION EFFECT

Humans have a strong tendency to assume that others are similar to themselves.

Expand your perception. Get beyond the halo effect to readdress a co-worker or acquaintance. Work to develop an understanding of this person and convince not only yourself but someone else of the value of getting beyond first impressions.

If you like steak, you tend to think that others also like steak. If you like a painting, you may assume that another person also would love to have it hanging on the wall.

Of course, that isn't necessarily so.

In business, misuse of the projection effect might have been responsible for a dismaying 70 percent failure rate among corporate mergers.

What happens is that the managers of one company tend to project their management philosophy and operating system onto the companies with which they merge or which they acquire. But if the other company, in fact, has different process-es, routines and philosophies, the two may not be compatible.

It's also one of the ground rules in advertising and public relations. Just because a product or an advertising approach works well with one market, doesn't mean it will with anoth-er. The Coca-Cola company found this out when it decided to distribute a red wine.

Company strategists knew that they had developed a suc-cessful marketing strategy for beverages over the years. They thought they would simply apply those tried-and-true methods to the new product. After two years and many millions of dollars in red ink, the company dropped its wine product. It had become all too clear that people don't drink red wine like they drink soft drinks. The two markets were profoundly different, and to sell the wine effectively would mean developing an entirely new promotion strategy. Eventually the company sold its winery.

If you're going to use the projection effect in your per-sonal relationships, be sure to speculate on and test the emotions and intentions of others. There always are those who would pretend to be open and sincere but are actually hiding their true natures. They may project an image that they believe will be appealing to you, but over time they will give themselves away. You must be ready to pick up the sig-nals through a person's revealed behavior and not take behavior at surface value. Listen and observe.

Here's something else to look out for. It's a bit like an inversion of the well-known Golden Rule:

Don't do unto others what you don't want others to do unto you. And don't impose on others what you want for yourself.

About 4,000 years ago, in China, ruled a wise and highly respected emperor, Yao. One day Emperor Yao visited Far Mountain, where the people welcomed him with blessings and wished Yao longevity, wealth and many children. Yao politely refused their wishes. The people of Far Mountain were puzzled. They said, "Long life, wealth and many children are what all people desire. Why are you not interested?"

Yao said, "Too many children lead to too many worries, too much wealth to too many trou-bles, and longevity invites insults. These three things will not help me cultivate my mind."

The people of Far Mountain had projected their own desires onto the Emperor, but he was an exception to the ways they knew. This story reminds us not to project our own judgments, nor force what we wish for ourselves onto others.

The first part of this rule is obvious enough. If something irritates or bothers you, don't do it to somebody else.

The second statement requires some contemplation. Different people have different likes and dislikes. Just because you like something or wish an event to occur, you cannot assume that anybody else will. A classic example is the person who throws a surprise party for her friend's birthday because she can't think of anything that would be more fun for her own birthday — and then is surprised when the friend is embarrassed and ill-at-ease. On a personal level, this is why it's not a good practice to give art as a gift and expect the recipient to hang it in his or her home. Their tastes in art may be different from yours.

PROXIMITY THEORY

People are more likely to develop good friendships or intimacy when they live close together rather than when they live far apart.

Contrary to the common saying, it is not absence but nearness that makes the heart grow fonder. Studies show that a higher percentage of good grades in a class go to students who sit close to the teacher.

There is a Chinese saying: "Water miles away can't put out a fire over here." Cultivate friendship with those in close proximity to you. They're the ones you'll call on in an emergency.

Don't make enemies of your neighbors. Most wars involve countries with common borders.

The application of this theory to the workplace is fairly obvious. It's important to get along well with the people you see every day. Moreover, if you hope for a quick promotion, try to place yourself near the people who most represent your company's power. Seek projects that let you work close to your boss. If your performance is good, your name will come to mind when it's time to promote someone.

Likewise, if your customers are important to you, stay close to them. Keep in regular contact. Call them, write them, send them birthday cards. That way when they need products or services, they'll think of you. To include others in your habitual domain or to be included in theirs, proximity is important.

Don't do unto others what you don't want others to do unto you. But don't impose on others what you want for yourself.

Corporate mergers often fail because one company projects a management philosophy and operating system onto another company that has different processes, routines and philosophies. Projecting can be damaging to personal relationships too.

During one work day, keep a record of the people with whom you are most friendly. Do these relationships prove or disprove the proximity theory? Is this helpful or harmful in your workplace?

RECIPROCATION

People tend to like others whom they know like them, and dislike those whom they perceive dislike them.

This should come as no surprise to you. In fact, examples of this kind of reciprocity are everywhere. We wish — or feel obligated — to extend to others the kind of behavior they extend to us. Favors are expected to be returned.

When you send a holiday card, you expect one in return.

If I scratch your back, will you scratch mine?

Fast-trackers who become managers or corporate officers at a relatively young age usually are very good at applying this behavior. They're willing to help departments other than their own or people in other divisions or companies. In return, they can often call on those whom they have helped for assistance.

This arrangement may benefit the individual, but it also builds teamwork within an overall operation. Various persons and departments find themselves working together for a common goal. Reciprocity is important to building friendships, organizations and even whole communities. From neighborhood baby-sitting cooperatives to public/private partnerships, modern communities need reciprocity to thrive.

In your relationships, always be alert for bribery or corruption. The line between appropriate examples of reciprocity and those that are illegal or immoral may be thin.

For your individual application of reciprocity, if someone does not like you, try to remain fair and impartial in your dealings with that person. If you can persistently like those who dislike you, over time you may be able to bring about a positive change in their attitude.

Also, remember to be careful not to let the value of the reciprocation be lost in guilt. Feeling guilty that you didn't return a favor — or that you don't like someone who likes you — sets up a negative charge structure. This is unhealthy and needs to be released. Reciprocity can enlarge your habitual domain, but guilt is not helpful.

Consider people you know from your office, school class, club or worship group. Choose three you would like to work with on a group project. Why did you choose those three? Now choose three you would not want to work with and explain the reasons why. Look again at the three you did not choose first and list good points about these people. Does this help change your attitude about them?

SIMILARITY EFFECT

People with similar backgrounds, attitudes and thought processes are more likely to develop good friendships and intimacy among themselves than with people who have different backgrounds and attitudes.

If everyone in your office wears business attire, you might regard someone in casual clothing as an outsider. "Not one of us."

A teenager will more than likely prefer to hang out with other teenagers rather than people her parents' age. Members of a particular religious denomination may find their closest friends within that group.

Cats prefer to socialize with other cats; dogs with other dogs.

The similarity effect has been well explored in the field of marketing, where various consumer groups are identified by age, income, geography, education — even the kind of cars they drive. This market segmentation allows the marketing of special products to specific groups.

Many successful corporations instill similar interests in their employees by letting those workers know what the company's goals are and the methods for achieving them. When people understand their common goals and have a common strategy to follow, they feel closer to one another.

Relationships built on similarity readily add to your habitual domain because you are already comfortable with some aspect of the other persons and less resistant to their ideas than you might be to those of strangers. On the other hand, be aware of the limitations of this tendency, because it can keep you from experiencing the advantages of diversity.

The common behavior tendency of similarity claims that human beings are more likely to develop close relationships with people who are similar to us than people with different backgrounds. This is another way of saying we are more comfortable with what we know. Yet if we wish to be growing, self-actualized people, should we choose to know people who are different from ourselves so we can continue to grow beyond our comfort zones?

SCAPEGOATING

When people are in a frustrated or anxious state and do not know the source of their frustration (or perhaps they do know but do not dare attack it directly), they often search for a substitute to attack in hopes of releasing their frustration. That substitute is a scapegoat.

Scapegoating, then, is a way of releasing a charge which we cannot quite identify. Unable to identify the real source of our charge, we pick a scapegoat to attack. The Nazi persecution of the Jews is one of history's most alarming examples.

Quite aside from the fundamental immorality of blaming someone unfairly, scapegoating has long-term negative consequences that far outweigh the quick, temporary relief the practice provides. We must:

All creatures prefer the company of similar creatures. Humans, however, can understand the value of diversity.

- Realize that scapegoating behavior is aggressive, irresponsible and crude. It is inherently unjust.
- Find the courage to face the source of our frustration. This may be very difficult, but the only way out is to find the source, confront it and solve the problem. Otherwise the problem may grow. If we can find the courage to do this, we will also gain more self-confidence.
- Protect ourselves against scapegoating. Since scapegoating is a least-resistance method of releasing frustration, ensure that our position and reputation is such that we are a high-resistance target.
- In corporations, develop a system of internal arbitration and a grievance procedure. This channel will allow people to vent their frustrations and be heard, thus lessening the likelihood that they will resort to scapegoating.

Recognizing our own tendencies to find a scapegoat for frustration can be the first step to building a habitual domain in which that kind of negative behavior has no place.

RESPONSIBILITY DIFFUSION IN GROUP BEHAVIOR

When we are members of a group and we lack precise and clear individual responsibilities, some of us tend to neglect the duties we otherwise would assume.

We figure that our slacking off will be compensated for by the efforts of the other group members. In other words, without specific responsibilities we believe our duties are diffused and shared with other group members.

Responsibility diffusion also suggests that should the project go well, all will share in the praise. Should it go badly, no one individual will be singled out for blame, but the responsibility for the failure will be shared by all group members.

In applying this behavior to groups, please remember:

- Clear and accountable responsibilities and authority should be granted to each individual. This will reduce diffusion of responsibility.
- We must cultivate good attitudes within the group: mutual concern and assistance, fairness, hard work,

An American travels to a foreign country with a different language than English, but the American speaks only English. Will the American quickly be able to form an opinion on whether the locals are friendly? How will behavior be affected on both sides?

Once there was a hermit who lived on a mountain. Every morning he got up early and raised the window just before the sun came up. In time, his opening the window and seeing the sun rise were linked in his mind, and he began to refuse the offers of friends to come down from the mountain to visit. "I have a responsibility," he said. "If I do not raise my window the sun may not rise."

The opposite of responsibility diffusion can be one person's assuming too much responsibility. Finding an appropriate balance of responsible action is an important part of understanding your own behavior.

41

Watch your workplace or some other organization (club, church) and see how the members diffuse responsibility. Do the members purposely disregard their responsibility? What are some ways to stop this behavior?

observation of the rules and positive attitudes for resolving conflicts. This reduces irresponsible behavior.

• In a group job, the responsibility of each individual should be made clear. When there is a problem, the relevant individuals should be held responsible.

• We must be able to identify wrong group behavior and be willing to oppose it. Just because it's a majority opinion, it isn't necessarily right.

• We have to apply this behavior very skillfully and carefully. Group behavior can create tremendous force and momentum — enough to overthrow a government. The unification of a group in protests and marches can be so effective that it will drive others to conform and support a cause. When their enthusiasm becomes so strong that they forget about the danger or their fear of death, they can achieve virtually any political or social reform.

For individuals, there is a difference in the ability to expand one's habitual domain and the willingness to let group behavior stand in for personal responsibility or choice. "Going along with the crowd" doesn't really tap our personal potential.

These eight strong behavior tendencies are common but they are not the only ones that are readily recognizable. Can you locate more that are frequently activated (*i.e.*, strong circuit patterns) to affect your thought and behavior? Try it.

As you begin to see behavior tendencies in yourself and others, you will observe basic human paradoxes as well.

A Few Basic Human Paradoxes

- We're usually unaware of the wonderful machines that are our bodies and brains — until they're broken.
- We usually take good for granted, and don't really appreciate what we have until it is threatened.
- We tend to be most impolite to the people who love us most — our parents.
- Suffering is a kind of charge; though unpleasant, it often makes us better people.
- People tend to underestimate the value of their invisible assets — skills, knowledge, talents — while overvaluing what they don't have.
- In the long run, losing may be better for you than winning. That's because losing creates a high level of charge which triggers a positive readjustment of your goal setting. Winning may leave you self-satisfied and without further goals to encourage your growth.
- It's easier to criticize, condemn and complain than it is to be appreciative, understanding and forgiving.
- People tend to select information consistent with their own views rather than that which does not conform to their beliefs. Positive feedback is more welcome than negative feedback — though negative feedback forces us to grow.
- Memories of anger and resentment tend to outweigh those of gratitude and appreciation. Moreover, we tend to think that how much we give outweighs how much we receive.

Recognizing these paradoxes can help us set aside the conflicts they represent and move ahead to create positive relationships with others and within ourselves, so we make the most of our limitless power and individual capabilities.

準備去劃出您的習慣領域

44

Chapter 4

Preparing to Map Your Habitual Domain

A s you read this book, you may decide to set any number of goals for yourself. The book itself has three very basic goals:

• To help you understand that your brain power — and therefore, your personal potential — is unlimited.
• To help you discover your habitual domain and ways to expand it.
• To help you discover how the habitual domains of others — individually and in organizations — can contribute productively to your efforts to reach your personal potential.

As you move ahead in the book, you will see how to estimate and assess personal and organizational habitual domains. Just about everyone can already perform this kind of assessment, at least on a superficial level. We do it as part of our regular orientation to the world and people around us, but most people do not see the fundamental and repeated patterns that would allow them to use their assessments to the best advantage.

智慧

游伯龍

低深領域理交換
對立陰陽永循環
內聯乾坤觀變化
矛盾促生追裂痕
空無境界外無空

Most importantly, most people are not aware of their own habitual domains. Assessing those should come first. But the tools to do this require some insights into some underlying principles of human knowledge. I call these the "Nine Principles of Deep Knowledge."

Nine Principles of Deep Knowledge

Certainly, these are simplifications of very complex circuit patterns. I have suggested images that might help you remember the principles easily. They are overviews, but broad views and assessments can be useful. In war, the generals on both sides think they can win (otherwise, a good general would avoid the war altogether). But it is the side which best assesses the overall situation that claims victory.

These principles represent some **operators** (thinking procedures and attitudes) that can produce better assessments. These operators can be used to understand your habitual domain and to expand it.

The operators, once they are pointed out to you, will seem obvious. But the person who can repeatedly use and master them will have a distinct advantage.

Recall that your actual domain is only a small portion of your potential domain, and only a small part of your actual domain is observable. Just because you can't observe it readily doesn't mean that it isn't in use: A runner can't see his calf muscle, but can't run without it.

We must examine the observable part of our actual domain, considering what we do know about ourselves, and from it glean as much information as possible about the entire actual domain and the potential domain as well.

The following nine principles can help us sharpen our assessment and, in the process, expand our habitual domains. Study them. Think about them. Make them strong circuit patterns in your brain so that you will automatically apply these principles to the events in your life.

THE DEEP AND DOWN PRINCIPLE

This can also be remembered as the **ocean principle**

Wisdom

- In the domain of **deep and down**, reasoning is **alternating.**
- Yin and Yang are **contrast and complement**; they are **revolving and cycling**.
- **Inner connecting** to the sky and the earth, **changing and transforming** can be observed.
- **Contradiction** can enrich life; look for **cracking and ripping.**
- Outside the true **void** state is not void.

(*translation of poem, page 46*)

知止，而后有定，定而后能静，静而后能安，安而后能虑，虑而后能得。

48

because water in an ocean ebbs and flows. Sometimes the tide is high, sometimes the sea retreats from shore. So it is with our energies and charges.

This principle has two meanings.

First, every so often you need to reduce your charges to as low a level as possible. When you're very busy and deeply concentrating, only ideas carrying extremely strong charges will occupy your mind. You simply will be too preoccupied with those situations to consider anything else.

Under such circumstances, ideas with lower charges (*i.e.*, the ideas corresponding to weak circuit patterns that can be activated only when our charge structure is at a lower level) cannot capture your attention. It may be that these low-charge ideas could be very valuable in solving the problem you're dealing with, but they just can't make themselves heard in the high-charged atmosphere of your mind.

There's another drawback to being consumed by high-charge ideas. If you have several of these demanding charges occupying your mind, your attention will be pulled back and forth among them. Your focus repeatedly will be turned on and off, without your ever being able to apply your intense and persistent focus to any one event.

Deep knowledge is hard to come by under these circumstances.

What's needed is a daily period of time — no matter how short — to practice deep thinking. It might be a period of quiet meditation or prayer, a relaxation exercise, soaking in a warm bath, running or hiking or simply sitting still and appreciating nature.

The idea is to empty your mind of desires and to insulate yourself from the external bombardment of ideas. By doing so you create an atmosphere conducive to deep thinking.

When you're relaxing, your overall charge level is lower, and "hidden" thoughts with much lower charges come bubbling up. Relaxation can also make you more sensitive to emerging problems, allowing you to solve them when they are at a fairly simple stage.

During a busy day, these weaker charges would never be able to make themselves known. In a relaxed situation, you can become aware of them.

Knowing when to stop produces calmness;
After calmness, tranquility can arrive;
After tranquility, inner peace can be achieved;
With inner peace, deliberation can be effective,
Which leads to the attainment of goals.
— Confucius
(translation of poem, page 48)

And you need to be aware of them if you're going to get the big picture. Individuals who never allow themselves to enjoy a rested state, those who race from morning to bedtime, will miss a lot.

Many relaxation exercises, even brief ones, can help you change your energy flow and help you get into deeper thought. A few moments can transform your "ocean feeling" from crashing waves to a steady tide of creative thought. Try this exercise next time you feel that your head is too full to think clearly.

The Sun Exercise

Stand in a relaxed way or sit in a comfortable chair. Hold your arms in front of you with your hands cupped gently upward as if you were holding in each palm a tiny, brilliant sun. Raise your arms until your hands are level with your head, bringing your arms to either side of your body and turning your palms toward your face so that the little suns can warm you.

Breathe in a deep and relaxed way and close your eyes. Feel the suns warming your face, as if you were lying on a tropical beach. Move your arms so that the suns warm your whole face and the top of your head. Gradually move your arms so that the suns can warm your neck and chest.

Feel the sun soaking into your muscles, soaking deeper into the cells of your body. Imagine every cell is drenched in sunlight. Move your arms to sun yourself down through your midsection and further onto your legs. If you are standing, sun your back at waist level. Feel the relaxation basking in the sun brings.

Do this for a few minutes every day and experience well-being. Do it when you are stressed and be revitalized.

A woman who is the president of a large department store in Taiwan, and a student of Habitual Domains, uses this exercise daily. She says that her work requires her to put so much energy into people every day that she was drained. Now she does this exercise before work and feels that she is able to radiate the warmth and energy of two suns to all the people who ask for her attention.

The *second* element of the Deep and Down Principle is regularly to take what I refer to as "the humble position" when dealing with others.

It's natural for human beings to cultivate a sense of superiority over their fellows. But periodically we need to drop the attitude of the teacher and view ourselves as students, to forget for the moment that we're the boss and take the unassuming position of an employee, or to let go of the parent role and see ourselves as children.

Many believe that assuming the inferior position in a situation is a sign of weakness. On the contrary — it is a regular practice of wise and secure individuals.

When we practice humility — asking for advice instead of giving it, taking orders instead of giving them — we actually strengthen our position.

Others will be flattered when we ask them to teach us, and any resentments they harbor toward us will begin to dissipate. As our teachers, they will feel a degree of responsibility toward us. In the role of students we're less likely to give offense and we gain the sympathy, understanding and support of others.

Moreover, when we assume the humble position, we force our minds to be open and willing to absorb new information.

Alternate all your assumptions about a particular set of problems to create an infinite number of good ideas.

THE ALTERNATING PRINCIPLE

This can be remembered as the **door principle**. A door can be open or shut. If it did not have this alternating function, it would have no value as a door. A door which is always closed or always open will lose its use as a door.

An assumption which is always imposed or always left out will lose its value as an assumption.

The alternating principle is simple: Sometimes we have to omit or change our combined assumptions so that we can create new ideas from different sets of assumptions.

It is easy to think of examples of how varying the combination of elements can create beneficial results. Chefs use this principle whenever they improve upon a dish by changing some of the flavors in it.

Another example: By combining 0 and 1 in different orders, mathematicians can create numerical systems and digital systems upon which electronic devices and computers are based.

Different combinations of the three primary colors (red, blue and yellow) can create an unlimited variety of colors and patterns. By alternating seven basic tones, one can compose an infinite number of songs.

Here's a business-based example of the door principle:

You may decide that a customer who complains a great deal about your company's products or services is a real pain. Your salesman may try to spend as little time with that customer as possible.

But instead of declaring, "A customer who complains is bad," change your assumption to this: "A customer who complains is good. In fact, that's the best kind of customer to have."

What happens when you act on that new assumption? For starters, if the complaining customer is to be considered a good customer, then you'd better start treating him like a good customer. Go out of your way to cater to his needs.

Treat him with particular deference. Listen carefully to those complaints that used to bother you — you'll probably pick up many tips on how to improve your products and services.

In other words, don't shy away from the customer who complains — embrace him. He'll tell you many things you need to know. Alternating your perception of the customer opens many new possibilities.

THE CONTRASTING AND COMPLEMENTING PRINCIPLE

This can be remembered as the **house principle**. A house offers barriers — a roof and walls against the weather — and also, contrasting with and complementing this quality, it has open space within.

Our lives are filled with ideas that contrast and complement each other.

Knowing and not knowing. Existence and nonexistence. Good and bad. Male and female. Old and young.

The list could go on indefinitely.

This is the paradox of knowledge: The wise person understands how little he or she knows. When we really open up our minds we understand that if we aren't aware of how much we don't know, we don't really know anything. We realize that if we don't know evil, we can't recognize good. If we haven't experienced sadness, we cannot truly experience joy.

What we see as existing contrasts with what is nonexistent. Meditate on this principle in peace for at least 15 minutes to explore the nonexistent and refresh your HD with insight. Listen to what you don't hear and see what you don't see.

Why is the ocean king of a hundred rivers?
Because it lies below them.
Therefore it is king of a hundred rivers.
— Lao Tzu

53

Without the known, the unknown is hard to define; without knowing the unknown, the known is not truly known.

Even what we see as existing can be contrasted with that which doesn't exist, and these two things complement each other in their functions. The ancient proverb says, "To light a candle is to cast a shadow."

Here's a pragmatic example. Take the room you now occupy. The walls, floor and ceiling that surround you are useless if not for the empty or "nonexistent" space that fills them. If the room was filled with concrete and had no open space, it would be useless as a room.

As it is, the walls, ceiling and floor provide protection and definition for the nonexistent space; yet it is the nonexistent space that makes the room useful.

Learn to look beyond just one element of the equation. Whenever you deal with a new event or idea, try to recognize also the corresponding contrasting and complementing events and ideas.

THE REVOLVING AND CYCLING PRINCIPLE

This principle can be remembered as **falling flower seeds**. When a flower fades in the autumn and falls to the ground, it carries with it the seeds for renewal in the following spring.

Every living thing is born to grow, reach a peak and die. This is the natural **Revolving and Cycling Principle** of biological organisms.

The earth itself experiences the revolving and cycling of the four seasons: spring, summer, fall, winter.

Even corporations go through life cycles consisting of ups and downs. A new product is established and sales accelerate. Later sales stabilize and, in time, decrease in the face of competition and newer products.

All people undergo cycles in their professional lives, in the state of their bodies and in their emotional makeup.

It's only natural. In fact, if you encounter someone who is always depressingly down or always giddily up, it's a sure sign that there's something wrong with that person's mental and emotional makeup.

An awareness of the Revolving and Cycling Principle can be useful in a variety of ways. For example, before beginning

To light a candle is to cast a shadow.

54

negotiations with a company, it would be useful to understand the cyclical nature of that firm's business and which phase of that cycle the firm now occupies.

If you make a proposal to someone and it is refused, don't give up hope. It's possible that the individual was in a particular low phase of his own internal cycle that leads him to reject new ideas. Wait a while and try again — you may catch him in a "high" state.

Lives and fortunes go in cycles, too. When you seem to be at the bottom, it means you're due to begin rising once again to the top. Just as each success contains the seeds of failure, so each failure contains the seeds of success.

The great inventor Thomas Edison was once asked by a reporter if he never became discouraged by his many initial failures to perfect a light bulb. Edison replied: "I have never failed. I merely discovered many methods for not creating an electric bulb."

Life is like a roller coaster and we all experience the ups and downs of its cycles. Look for the cycles in your daily, weekly, monthly and yearly life to learn more about yourself and your environment. Look for the seeds of failure in every success and the seeds of success in every failure. When can you use this principle next?

THE INNER CONNECTION PRINCIPLE

This is the **blood is thicker than water principle**. It means, simply, that a close connection will be honored over simple acquaintance.

You may have heard the old saying about never judging another person until you've walked a mile in their shoes.

The thought behind the adage is also the basis of the **Inner Connection Principle**. The idea is to build as many strong channels as possible connecting us to the inner core of another individual's habitual domain. The process is often called "bonding." When this occurs, you will be able to strongly identify with that individual and be better able to predict his behavior and influence him.

Politicians tend to be extremely good at building these inner connections. If you ever attend a political rally, watch the activities of the candidates. They will recognize individuals in the crowd and make gestures or comments to show that they are aware of the presence of those "special" people. Those individuals are gratified; they feel they have an inner connection with someone as important as a governor, senator or president.

Effective politicians really work at building this connection. They know the key to their election is to make many

Who are your closest friends? Remember when you first met and developed your foundation of friendship, what steps or stages you went through. How did you learn about each other?

other people feel like a vital part of their cause.

This principle has numerous business applications. For example, how do you build connections with your customers? It's obvious: You try to put yourself in their shoes, to understand what they need, to sense how they feel about your product or service. For one corporation to understand and affect another requires understanding the core habitual domain of the organization and the ability to build up as many strong connections as possible.

People with good instincts and common sense may constantly be forging inner connections with others without even realizing it. The referral system, alumni organizations, clubs, trade associations can all be useful channels for connections. Making inner connections is the real goal of what is sometimes called "networking."

Think about yesterday. Imagine how everyone with whom you came in contact might affect your life.

THE CHANGING AND TRANSFORMING PRINCIPLE

This is the *ice and steam principle*. The world is constantly changing, and so are the habitual domains of the individuals and organizations that inhabit it. They change when circumstances (or parameters) make them.

Water will transform into steam or ice when its temperature (a parameter) is drastically changed. Indeed, when relative parameters change drastically in many realms — not just in nature — new things, substances or forms will emerge.

Suppose a friend's income doubles overnight. Or is cut in half. Can you envision how his lifestyle, his personality, his habitual domain will change?

A small shop that grows to be a large corporation not only undergoes change in the amount of business it handles, but in its organizational structure. A business with thousands of employees has different needs from one with a dozen or so workers.

A person who has been in the same job for years and believes he knows all there is to know about it could find himself being pushed aside by someone coming with new and fresh ideas.

Businesses that are willing to change are businesses with a better chance of surviving.

Take as an example the direct sales company which for

years had opened every day at 8 a.m. and closed at 6 p.m. But a new CEO had an idea for improving customer service and increasing sales. He offered special incentives to phone order operators who would come in an hour early or work an hour later.

The CEO realized that many of the company's customers might prefer to place their orders before going to work in the morning or after coming home in the afternoon. By expanding the hours of operation, the company sold more and kept customers happier.

People who are willing to change are people with a better chance for happiness and success. We must all be on the alert for changes and their implications and be willing to change ourselves. If we do not, we will never tap our potential.

Can you name someone who has greatly changed or expanded his or her habitual domain in the last few years?

CONTRADICTION PRINCIPLE

This is the **stand on your head principle**. Sometimes it is worth seeing the world upside down, or at least from a different angle; it can clear your mind.

To use the **Contradiction Principle** we need to look at an event from the other way around. We must find out if there is an event or information that contradicts our conclusions. If there is, then we must revise our assumptions or change our conclusions.

This can work two ways. One is to take a different perspective to a problem or challenge. The phrase "thinking outside the box" refers to this approach, which is a mainstay for artists, designers, writers, advertising executives and others in "creative" businesses.

Applying the Contradiction Principle to our daily thinking can sharpen our perceptions to observe greater detail and can enrich our thought processes. Some of the best tools for creative thinking involve using contradictions, saying "what if" to the ordinary.

Using contradiction effectively can also mean taking a second look, examining events, processes, relationships more closely. Maybe your company expects to buy a product for a particular price, then discovers the price is much more. This contradiction between expectation and reality causes you to look for other vendors — and to expand your habitual domain in the process.

THE CRACKING AND RIPPING PRINCIPLE

This is the ***broken teacup principle***. A teacup may have a hairline crack that is not even visible as the cup sits on the shelf. But when you pour hot water into it, the cup will leak, or even shatter.

Cracks are the weak point of any structure. If you want to destroy a mighty fortress, you can do so by working on its crack lines and ripping them open.

If you would save the fortress, you must repair and fill up the cracks.

A habitual domain consists of a series of subsystems. Conflicts and inconsistencies among these subsystems are inevitable. In business, if you want to break the habitual domain of a competitor, you must observe carefully and determine where the cracks — the inconsistencies and conflicts — exist. Then you must decide what can be done to break open those cracks.

At the same time you should be aware of the cracks in your own habitual domain. These cracks may need patching. Or, you may determine that your old habitual domain needs breaking down and rebuilding (just as the "desktop" on your computer may need rebuilding occasionally).

In our personal habitual domains, these cracks can be old fears, inflexible modes of thinking, grudges or any other "habits" that keep us from positive change and growth. Whenever you find yourself justifying a thought or behavior with the premise that you have "always done it this way," it may be time to see if that behavior represents a crack in your habitual domain.

Here's an example of **Cracking and Ripping** in business. Let's say your company sells computers. Another company sells computers as well. But you discover that the competition has a cracking line: While they sell good computers at a reasonable price, they are not very good about servicing the units already sold.

That's where you attack your competition — by making sure that your after-sales service is the best possible. You've identified the cracking line. Now you can rip them apart.

Of course, if the competition is smart they'll be looking for the cracks in *your* operation. It's up to you to do some self-analysis and discover the weak points before they do.

Make a list of ideas that have become habituated over time in your HD. These ideas might be the value of one political party over another, the need for business clothing at the office, the value of spring cleaning, the need to go to your mother-in-law's for dinner every Sunday. Step back from each of the ideas on your list and examine their relevance to your situation today.

Your habitual domain is like the earth — strong but full of seams where new layers have been added.

THE VOID PRINCIPLE

This might be called the ***empty space principle***. We all tend to think in terms of our own habitual domains, and we tend to think that anything outside our own habitual domains doesn't really exist.

Rather than being on the hunt for new ideas and concepts, we find it's more convenient and easier to use the same sets of concepts over and over throughout our lives. Our habitual domains are self-perpetuating in this way.

The **Void Principle** simply states that the outside of our habitual domains is not empty. Just because we don't perceive it or recognize it doesn't mean it isn't there. And whether we acknowledge it or not, those other HDs can have a profound effect on us.

When an event occurs outside the comprehension of their habitual domains, individuals who see everything outside themselves as a void become bewildered. They cannot respond effectively.

To avoid becoming confused or defensive (and thus miss out on useful or desirable ideas), we need to expand our habitual domains continuously by absorbing what we can of others'. We must regularly let go of some of our own habitual domains so as to empty them of prejudices and make them capable of absorbing new habitual domains. If you apply the Void Principle in the sense that you make a void, or empty place, in your domains, then you can use another of the principles for deep knowledge to fill that void with new information.

For example, perhaps you have a problem at work that you cannot seem to solve alone. You empty out of your habitual domain the idea that you must solve the problem yourself in order to show your competence. You use the Deep and Down Principle's lessons about humility and you approach a co-worker for help and advice. Together you find a solution. You have now not only solved your problem, you have a habitual domain that has broadened to include the new idea that

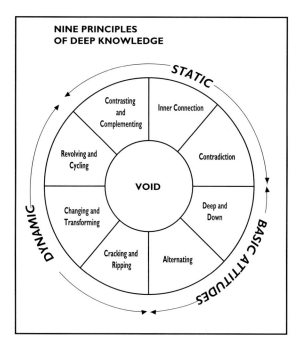

NINE PRINCIPLES OF DEEP KNOWLEDGE

STATIC

Contrasting and Complementing

Inner Connection

Revolving and Cycling

Contradiction

VOID

Changing and Transforming

Deep and Down

Cracking and Ripping

Alternating

DYNAMIC

BASIC ATTITUDES

When you are trying to reach a deeper level of knowledge, apply the void principle first, letting go of your preconceived ideas and emptying your mind. Then use other principles to fill the void with new information. Consider principles related to your basic attitudes, but also principles that are static and dynamic by nature.

competence can mean asking for help at the right time.

When our habitual domain is capable of identifying with the HDs of every other person and organization on earth, we'll have reached a true "void" state in which nothing is unknown to us, yet we know what is unknown to others. This state of enlightenment has been the goal of many spiritual thinkers throughout history. For most humans, it can never be reached. But as a goal, it has infinite value to help us grow and expand our capabilities to understand.

In a less cosmic way, Napoleon's career shows an example of the void principle. He thought himself such a superior military strategist that he refused to even consider the existence of the habitual domain of his opposing generals until it was too late.

A wise general likes to attack outside his enemy's HD. The bewilderment of the enemy provides the window of opportunity for victory.

Think of some inventions and advances in science, medicine, engineering, art that have been the result of HD expansions by individuals and have contributed to HD expansions of others. Imagine a world in which there is no HD expansion.

Alinsky's Strategy in Chicago

A terrific example of the Void Principle occurred when social activist Saul Alinsky was asked to help the black community of Chicago solve a problem. In 1960 African Americans living in Chicago had little political power and were subject to discriminatory treatment in just about every aspect of their lives.

Leaders of the black community invited Alinsky, who was to become famous for his "blockbusting" method of integrating neighborhoods, to participate in their effort.

Alinsky clearly was aware of deep knowledge principles. Working with black leaders he came up with a strategy so alien to city leaders that they would be powerless to anticipate it.

His plan was simple, legal and incredibly effective: Several hundred African Americans would continuously occupy every public restroom in Chicago's massive O'Hare Airport.

At first glance that might seem like nothing more than an inconvenience. But consider: Thousands of individuals visit the airport daily, many of them visitors to Chicago. With every restroom occupied continuously, there would be no place for all these persons to relieve themselves.

Under these circumstances, children probably would be

the first to find release wherever they could. Adults would eventually be forced to follow.

Within hours O'Hare would smell terrible and become virtually unusable. Chicago would achieve instant notoriety around the world.

As it turned out, the plan never was put into operation. City leaders found out about Alinsky's strategy and, realizing their inability to prevent its implementation and its potential for damaging the city's reputation, met with black leaders and promised to fulfill several of their key demands.

Alinsky understood that Chicago's municipal government wasn't prepared to think of public restrooms as a battleground for racial equality. The plan was beyond the comprehension of their habitual domain.

Ancient Chinese wisdom reminds us that the usefulness of a wheel comes not only from the spokes but from the spaces between them. Much of your strength also comes from the "empty" places, the ideas not yet fully formed, that will permit your domain room to grow.

劃出您的習慣領域

Chapter 5

Mapping Your Habitual Domain

Just as snails carry their shells with them wherever they go, so humans carry their habitual domains — invisible, unwritten, unspoken; continuously, but for most people unconsciously affecting our decisions and behavior.

Through years of learning and experience we all gradually become "psychologists." We know roughly when and why people are happy or sad, enthusiastic or frustrated, angry or pleasant, especially people in relationships that are close to us. Even so, when it comes to describing precisely who we ourselves are, why we behave as we do, most of us cannot do it effectively, systematically and accurately.

Imagine yourself as an archaeologist, sifting through the remains of an ancient civilization. What do the materials you uncover say about these people, their institutions, their individual lives?

To understand yourself well, you need to become an archaeologist of your own habitual domain. You're going to delve into your own past, examining the events and people that shaped you. Once you understand why you are who you are, you can begin to address whatever parts of your personality and your life you want to change.

This is really a "workbook" chapter. You might wish to

The Master's Tale

A student approached the great Japanese martial arts master, Miyamoto Musashi, and requested to study with him.

"How long will it take me to learn martial arts?" the student asked.

"Ten years," said the master.

"Ten years is too long. My parents are old and could die before they witnessed my accomplishment. Suppose I double my efforts? Suppose I train doubly hard? Then how long would it take?" said the student.

"Twenty years," said Miyamoto Musashi.

"Why?" asked the student, very disappointed.

"A really fine martial artist keeps one eye looking out and one eye looking inward at all times," said the Master. "If you work twice as hard, say 16 hours a day, to perfect the outward forms, you will have no time for self-reflection and perfecting the inward forms. It would be impossible to grow to be great."

read it now and go on to reading the rest of this book, then return at your leisure to work through the thinking and reflection this chapter requests. At the end of this book are some worksheets you might duplicate and use to make your notes as you study yourself. Here are some recommendations for using this workbook chapter successfully:

- Keep a paper record of your progress. Don't just read this book; write down your responses. The very act of writing down key words and phrases will force you to address and remember the details of your life and point to ways for new inner explorations. Use the forms in the back of the book or make up your own.
- Take your time. Understanding your habitual domain is a lifelong process. Don't try to complete an assessment of your HD in one sitting. It can't be done. You're much too complicated for that.

This can be one of the most important activities you will ever undertake. Tackle the project a little at a time. Give yourself plenty of room for thought and rumination. Reflection is necessary for growth in your self-understanding, just the way rest is necessary for muscles to be built up effectively.

Every body builder knows to put a day or two between each heavy workout session because if muscles are not allowed to rest, they won't achieve maximum strength. Tapping your brain's potential and building your mind's power is no different. You won't achieve your maximum strength without time for reflection.

Basic Functions of Your Habitual Domain

You can understand your own habitual domain. Then you can use the same approach to evaluate the habitual domain of your family members, friends, loved ones, co-workers, business associates. Through practice and paying attention, you will develop proficiency in understanding other people's habitual domains. This will be of lifelong benefit to you.

All your interactions with others, from simple dinner table conversation at home to complex negotiations in your work, will be easier and more meaningful. Indeed, we can only begin to hope for peace between the people of the world when we are able to imagine and understand others' habitual domains.

To assess your own habitual domain, you will need to take a long look at yourself in the areas of these behavior functions:

- how your memory works
- your special knowledge and skills
- your physiological state
- how you set goals
- your state evaluation of the situation (how you evaluate your state of mind or situation)
- your charge structures
- your attention allocation
- your interaction with the world

One of the most common questions asked by those just starting to assess their own habitual domains centers on the qualities of the ideal habitual domain. Certainly, there can be no higher goal than to reach for an ideal habitual domain (we will talk about that in Chapter 10). But many beginning students of habitual domain are looking for speedy assessments.

Is it better to be introverted or extroverted? Should you rely more on thinking or feeling? Would you be better served with an optimistic or a pessimistic outlook? Should you strive for flexibility, or is consistency and dedication a better path to success?

Actually there are no speedy answers. Really understanding yourself is a marvelous, life-long process. And there are no right answers. Each person's habitual domain is unique, so there is no right or wrong set of characteristics.

There are, however, a couple of fundamental guides to behavior that can help you get the most benefit from a given situation.

The first is for the short term. In an intense situation, you may find that the best response is an extreme one.

If you're in the locker room preparing for a big game, you'll probably be better served by pumping up your emotions. Logical thinking is unlikely to do you much good on the playing field. If you are going to give a speech, a state of high anticipation is important — it keeps you focused and communicates itself to an audience as sincerity and enthusiasm.

For longer term circumstances, a steady moderation is more appropriate. A fever pitch can't be usefully sustained for long. For instance, a scientist conducting a complex study will want to approach it methodically. If he forgets his scientific approach and only does those experiments that appeal to him emotionally, his conclusions will be of little use.

If you can rate behavior on a scale of 1 to 10, there will be times when a very low response (a 1) is appropriate. At other times an extremely high response (a 10) will be required to deal with a particular situation.

In the long term, most people are probably happiest when the basic events in their lives are a 4, 5 or 6. A life that swings too far in one direction or another, a life made up entirely of 1s and 2s and 9s and 10s, is a life out of balance. If you take a long look at your overall behavior and find yourself regularly behaving or thinking in extremes, it may be time to step back and take stock of yourself. The ideal habitual domain is a state of equilibrium.

A MEMORY EXERCISE

Here is an exercise that will quickly allow you to learn a great deal about yourself.

Think back to your childhood before the age of five. Ask yourself two questions:

"Who were the individuals who had the most influence on my life?" There are at least three or four, including your parents, family members, neighbors, preschool teachers, perhaps even a favorite baby sitter.

"Which events most influenced me during this period of time?" These events can be both pleasurable and unpleasant. Summers spent on your grandparents' farm may have instilled in you a lifelong love of the outdoors. On the other hand, a traumatic illness that resulted in several weeks in the hospital could have left you with a lifelong dread of visiting the doctor.

Divide your life into three- to five-year segments (for example: the elementary school years, junior high, high

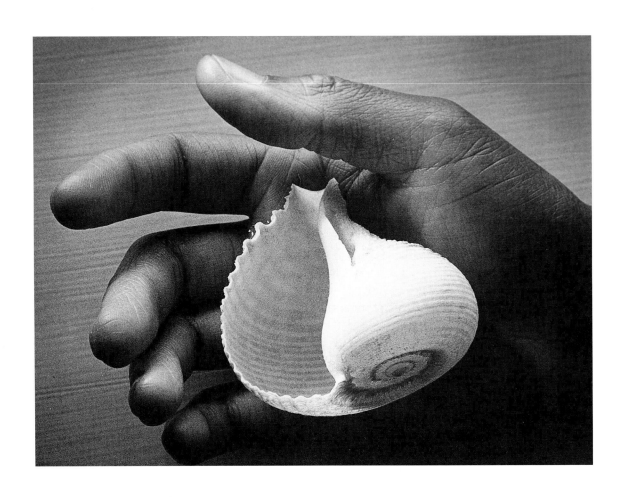

school, college, the first years of marriage etc.) and ask the same questions of these time periods.

Be honest with yourself. Don't ignore or gloss over negative experiences or individuals. Undoubtedly, they still exert a great deal of control over you.

Here's a true story that illustrates the effectiveness of this technique:

In one of my classes was a young woman who had an extremely hard time relating to her male teachers. She didn't like to engage them in conversation, she didn't participate in their classes and she was uneasy in their presence.

Her behavior soon came to my attention, and in a conference I asked her to go home and try this memory exercise.

She later reported that the exercise forced her to re-evaluate the influence of her father. This man was an alcoholic who, when drinking, often became violent and brutalized his family.

As a result of the strong circuit patterns these unpleasant experiences created in her brain, the young woman had a terrific fear and mistrust of all male authority figures.

The wonderful thing about this story is that once she recognized the source of her anxiety, this student made peace with her father and most of her fear disappeared. She had spent years trying *not* to face her unpleasant childhood memories, without realizing that those memories were nonetheless having a seriously debilitating effect on her life as an adult.

Time and time again you will find that the simple act of *recognizing* the source of a strong circuit pattern (in her case, fear of men in authority) is often enough to defuse that pattern, to change it to something more positive.

In the cross section of a tree trunk, or the lines on a shell, you can see how the growth occurs in stages, ring after ring. We can look at our HD development in this way. On a piece of paper draw a circle for each year of your life, one outside the other (or even just a 10-year period). In each ring, note major experiences and changes that occurred during each year. How did the experiences help your habitual domain to grow? Did you grow steadily or in spurts? Have you grown lately? Were tough times the periods of most growth?

HOW CIRCUIT PATTERNS WORK

While everyone's brain operates along the same basic lines, individual differences do exist. Just as we each have specific and complex ways of expressing ourselves and moving, so do the ways in which we record, store and retrieve our memories have an individual stamp. But very few of us have stopped to analyze just how our individual memories work.

Every memory is a circuit pattern. That pattern may be very strong, which means that you have no trouble retrieving it. It may be so strong, in fact, that it dominates your consciousness. You think about it all the time, whether you want to or not. This is particularly true of individuals who have undergone a traumatic experience. For instance, a person who has been a victim of crime often will find himself haunted daily by memories of those events.

On the other hand, your circuit pattern for a particular memory may be very weak. While it may be true that everything we see or experience remains stored in our brains, the patterns of some memories may be so weak that we cannot consciously recall them.

I tell my university students that after every class session they should review their notes as soon as possible. Having heard me lecture on a subject, their brains will have created a circuit pattern of the information I provided (if they were paying attention).

Initially, it will be only a weak circuit pattern, and it will grow weaker still if they do not reinforce it quickly.

This is the benefit of a prompt review. The circuit pattern or memory will be strengthened as it undergoes this form of mental exercise. Students who do not refer to the day's notes until the end of the semester are often frustrated to find that they can recall little of the original lesson. They go into their final exams with a distinct disadvantage.

This is true for business people as well. Reviewing meeting notes soon after a meeting can help put the conversations that occurred into active use. Meeting notes that go into a file drawer without review remain only notes.

A perfect example of how circuit patterns develop and grow stronger can be found in the study of foreign languages. Initially, students will find themselves mentally translating a foreign phrase into English. But with repeated use of that foreign language, the circuit patterns become so strong that students find themselves thinking in that language. They no longer have to *translate* a conversation into their native tongue to understand it.

In building circuit patterns, repetition is everything. Reinforcing circuit patterns regularly can have broad and lasting applications. A wise woman in my native Taiwan employed this truth to great success in her efforts to build a hospital.

Cheng Yen's Hospital

The Honorable Cheng Yen, a renowned Buddhist nun and a very revered figure in Taiwan, decided several years ago to build a hospital for the poor. She didn't have the money for this effort, but asked her several dozen followers to pledge $15 a month to the effort.

Rather than asking them to pay a lump sum of $15 a month, she told her supporters to donate 50 cents every day.

The actual amount of money being donated by these individuals would be the same, but the act of making a donation every day instead of just once a month had a ripple effect.

Many of Cheng Yen's followers were middle-aged women who frequented Taiwan's markets. In the course of their daily routines, they often would mention that they had to save 50 cents a day in order to do good deeds for Cheng Yen. Soon individuals from all walks of life became aware of the nun's efforts and themselves became supporters.

Here's the point: When a person donated 50 cents every day, the donating behavior was repeated every day. The circuit patterns for this charitable behavior thus grew stronger and stronger. In time, whenever a donor opened a wallet or purse, he or she was reminded of Cheng Yen's work. Simultaneously, their "pro-charity" circuit patterns were diffused among those they contacted through words and deeds.

Cheng Yen's strategy worked. Within a few months she had raised more than enough money to begin building her hospital.

MEMORY FUNCTIONS

Circuit patterns are central to a habitual domain. Circuit patterns are the key to changing our minds, thus changing our behavior, building more desirable behavior and expanding our habitual domains.

We all have different ways of **encoding** memory and **organizing** the information we receive every day.

For most of us, **visual images** and *pictures* are the most commonly used encoding devices. A majority of people are "visual learners," that is, they are most likely to remember something they see, rather than something they hear.

See if this story sounds familiar: You're in your bedroom one morning getting dressed, and you make a mental note to get a certain book off a shelf in the living room because you'll need it at work that day.

You finish dressing, eat breakfast, make sure the kids are dressed and you're ready to go out the door when you realize there was something you were going to take to work.

What was it? You can't remember. You wander from room to room wondering what object it was that you needed.

One thing you do remember: When the thought first occurred to you, you were in your bedroom, getting dressed. You might have been looking into your closet.

So you go to the bedroom, stand exactly where you were when you made that original mental note to yourself. You look into your closet and — presto! — suddenly it comes back to you. The book in the living room! Of course . . . !

At the moment while getting dressed that you made a mental note to get the book, you created a visually encoded circuit pattern. You were looking in the closet at that moment, and so the idea of "get the book" was cemented or piggy-backed to the visual stimulus of looking into your closet.

Visual stimulus is a very powerful memory tool. But there are certainly others. Persons with poor eyesight are especially sensitive to **sound, smell, taste** and **touch** as encoding devices.

Some encoding methods don't rely much on sensory input. For instance, some individuals employ **logical thinking** or **concentrate on certain words** to build memories.

In most cases, memories are strongest when the individual makes a special effort to encode the information. If you meet an individual named Baker and mentally make a picture of him wearing a baker's hat, it's likely that you'll remember this person's name the next time you meet.

How do you encode your information? Do you have to listen, see, smell, taste or touch before you build a strong impression or circuit patterns for certain things? How do you retrieve and make use of your stored memory?

The key to remembering is to exercise your memories. Use them and they will grow stronger. That stored information which you are aware of all the time — the names of your family members, for example — are memories that are retrieved repeatedly. The circuit patterns that represent those memories are not only extremely strong, but they have spread, diffusing throughout your brain and attaching themselves to other circuit patterns, making them easier still to recover.

What are your **most active memories** (*i.e.*, the core elements of your habitual domain)? These are the memories which continue to have tremendous influence on your lives.

These **core memories** may be extremely positive. The memory of an intense spiritual or religious experience can have a continually transforming effect on an individual's life. So can romantic love or memories of one's children.

A bad core memory also can have negative consequences. If your mind is dominated by fear or by a desperate need for revenge, it can prevent your enjoyment of life.

How **deep** and **detailed**, how **broad**, how **extensive** and how **integrated** is the memory? Did you decide to strengthen certain memories, while letting others lapse? How did you make those decisions?

Can you quickly shift from one set of memories to another? Can you turn from one task to another or do you function best with just one topic before you?

KNOWLEDGE AND SKILLS

Given some time to think about it, you can identify dozens of skills you possess. Many activities are complex sets of skills, like driving a car. You can speak, walk, tie a knot and make use of other common skills that most of us exhibit every day.

What about the **human skills** that allow you to deal with your fellow human beings? These allow you to know others, to work with them, to exhibit leadership or, conversely, to be an effective follower.

Think for a few minutes about these **interacting skills**. In conversation, are you a good listener? Or are you so preoccupied with what you're going to say next that you pay little attention to what others say? Can you approach any topic with an open mind, or are your feelings so established and rigid that you can tolerate little that goes against your feelings and beliefs?

Write down your main channels for encoding new information and how you store it. What makes you remember? When you encounter a new stimulus, how do you make yourself understand it quickly?

Are there memories that continuously occupy your mind or attention? Are they getting in the way of your growth and change?

Goal Functions

From studying the work of many psychologists, I created a list of seven basic **goal functions** shared by virtually every human. Can you think of others?

Normally we don't pay attention to these functions because our brains achieve these goals silently and naturally. But when we fail to reach these goals or keep them in equilibrium, we become uneasy and begin looking for ways to deal with this feeling.

If we are aware of these goal functions, they can be used to expand our habitual domains.

Survival and Security: These functions include physiological health and basic needs such as maintaining normal body temperature and blood pressure; quantity and quality of air and water; food, shelter, mobility, safety and the acquisition of wealth and goods.

Perpetuation of the Species: Sexual activities, reproduction, family love, health and welfare, nurturing others and being nurtured.

Feelings of Self-importance: Self-esteem and the respect of others; recognition and prestige; personal achievement; creativity; giving and accepting sympathy and protection; accumulation of wealth (beyond that required for simply survival and security).

Social Approval: Friendship; respect of others; affiliation with desired groups; conformity with group ideology, beliefs, attitudes and behaviors; giving and accepting sympathy and protection.

Sensuous Gratification: Sexual, visual, auditory, olfactory, taste, touch.

Cognitive Consistency and Curiosity: The desire for consistency in our beliefs, perceptions and behaviors; exploring the unknown.

Self-actualization: The ability to accept and depend on oneself, to stop identifying with others and to rely on one's own standards; to aspire to the "ego-ideal" and to detach oneself from social demands and customs when desirable.

You have **communication skills** that connect you with others. Can you express ideas clearly, effectively and persuasively? Are you better at doing this verbally or in writing? Do you speak, write or read in a foreign language?

Do you have strong **analytical skills**? Are you capable of logical thought or do your emotions tend to dictate your view of things?

Closely aligned with this are your **decision making skills**. Facing a problem, can you make decisions quickly and effectively? Do you embrace risk or avoid it? Do you opt more for rigid routines or flexibility? Once you make a decision, are you committed to it? Or are you open to altering a course of action if circumstances seem to require it?

And you have **professional skills**, the skills you have built up over years of education and experience. Imagine you're applying for a job and want to list the skills you will be able to provide to your new employer. Your abilities can probably be grouped under a general area such as accounting, marketing, management, engineering, writing, law, science, art, teaching. In that general area, you will have highly specialized skills, some that are unique to you.

How are your interacting skills? Can you open your mind? Can you open another person's mind so he or she can listen to you?

PHYSIOLOGICAL CONDITION

A huge part of each individual's overall habitual domain depends on matters of health. We barely think about it when we're feeling good, but just try writing a speech when you've got a splitting headache. You'll probably find that the headache will win — you'll have to give up working until it goes away.

We're always monitoring the conditions of our bodies, usually unconsciously. When our physiological system is working properly, it produces no charge and we're not even aware of it. But when one or more of our systems is out of order, or when illness occurs, it can create such a high level of charge that it dominates our minds and attention.

When we're sick we may not be able to endure the hardship of work. We are consumed by worries over our health and the effort to become well.

Do you pay attention to matters of health? Do you spend a significant amount of time to maintain a healthy body?

What do you do best? What do you want to do most?

SETTING YOUR GOALS

What are the **priorities** of your daily life? For some individuals, pleasure is everything. Their primary goal in life is to have a good time.

Others are so devoted to their careers that they have no time for other considerations — even their own families.

Or a parent may be so devoted to the goal of raising healthy, happy children that he or she de-emphasizes other goals, such as cultivating friendships with other adults or of gaining respect from the community.

Every day in dozens of ways we set goals for ourselves. A goal could be something as big as setting our sights on a promotion at the office. It could be as seemingly modest as getting to work on time.

In both cases, by setting a goal we have created a charge structure that stimulates us to take the actions and make the decisions that will bring the goal closer. It might mean putting in extra hours on the job to show the boss that we're worthy of that promotion. Or it could be as simple as deciding not to linger over the morning newspaper so that we can get a head start on rush hour traffic.

Of course, our goal setting is fluid and our goal priorities change —sometimes abruptly. If you wake up in the middle of the night and smell smoke, your overriding goal will be to get everyone out of the house safely. At a moment like that, the goals you have set for yourself at the office will be insignificant to you.

A Goal-Setting Exercise

On a piece of paper draw seven horizontal lines about 4 inches long. At the left end of each write the number 0; at the right end put down a 10. In the middle of the line, mark a 5.

Now use a line for each of the following priorities; mark on the line where you believe each falls. A 10 means that this is an extremely high priority for you. A 0 means you hardly care about that goal at all. A 5 puts you right in the middle.

Save your responses to this exercise and repeat it in a week or so. Have your priorities shifted during that time?

Another thing to remember: This isn't a test. There are no correct or incorrect answers. The idea is to be honest with yourself. If, after completing this exercise, you see aspects of your personal priorities that you're not happy with — so be it. You'll be in a position to change them.

Here are the goals to prioritize:

- **Survival**: If you're acutely worried about your health or falling into poverty, you might give survival a 10. If you really don't care — if in fact you court danger and enjoy it — you'll give yourself a much lower number. Survival and security include our physiological health and basic needs, such as proper quality and quantity of food, shelter, clothes, mobility, safety, acquisition of wealth or other economic considerations.

- **Perpetuation of the Species**: This includes sexual activities and romance, family love, health, welfare. All living organisms are programmed with the goal to perpetuate their species. How strong is your drive to have children? To protect your offspring? Younger people who believe they will have plenty of time in which to start a family might not place having children at the top end of their scale. A middle-aged woman who hears the ticking of her biological clock may give this category a 9 or a 10.

  Most parents place a very high priority on protecting their children. The safety of one's offspring can, and often does, supersede career, affluence, the desire for recognition and prestige, and a host of other usually dominant goals.

- **Feelings of Self-Importance**: We make a contribution to others if we can fulfill their need to feel important. Do you get enough of this in return from others? Is feeling good about yourself very important to you? Then give it a 9 or a 10. Are you a person who never even bothers to consider such things? Then you'll register in the low numbers.

- **Social Approval**: As social animals, humans have a natural need for social approval, recognition and belonging. If someone compliments you, you feel pleased, because your social approval need is partially satisfied for the moment. Some of us are tremendously concerned about how we are perceived by our peers and are

Think of how a specific event over which you had no control expanded your habitual domain. How were you changed?

more than willing to mold our behavior in order to please others. Others care less about fitting in. How do you rank yourself ?

- **Sensuous Satisfaction**: This includes the gratification of our senses, all of them. Good food, comfortable surroundings, an occasional massage or a soak in a hot bath. How important are these to you? At different points in our lives our goals in this category will change in importance to us.

- **Logical Consistency and Curiosity**: This is a basic instinct in human beings. We are curious about new things, but, at the same time, we don't like cognitive dissonance. We search for consistency in our beliefs, perceptions and behaviors. We distrust change, even when we crave it. We keep people who seem inconsistent (therefore, not trustworthy) at a distance. Are you bothered if you cannot see a steady, overriding pattern or logic to your behavior? Are you concerned when you find yourself engaged in contradictory behavior?

- **Self-Actualization**: This is a fundamental life goal. As a person matures, he or she will feel increasingly a need for self-actualization — a need to "become the person I always wanted to be." Sometimes, people make major career or life pattern shifts during middle age. These so-called "midlife crises" are often simply responses to the need for self-actualization. When reports of a person making a successful life shift are shared, most people feel intense interest, and sometimes envy.

In the process of self-actualization, a person wants independence and will often detach from peers' influence. The search for the meaning in life becomes more important, and a person will choose a direction and stick with what he believes to be true. Because religious systems can satisfy the human need for self-actualization, religion has become the most pervasive social system, culturally and financially, around the world.

A Goal-Setting Checklist

Now that you have ranked priorities for some fundamental goals, consider this checklist of some of the qualities that

How important is it to you to have a philosophy or frame of reference to count on?

What are your personal goals? Are these different from your goals at work? Are these goals conflicting?

can contribute to reaching your goals. How are you at applying these to your own priorities?

Coherence in your goal setting can help you avoid conflicts and move steadily toward your goal. It's obvious that to achieve one goal, you may have to sacrifice other goals. You can hardly achieve your goal of more relaxation time if another of your goals is to become CEO of your corporation. To address either goal is to undermine the other.

In such circumstances your goal setting lacks coherence. Your goals, taken as a whole, generate too much conflict and too many contradictions. Virtually all of us lack some coherence in our goal setting because we must address conflicting elements in our lives. For example, juggling job and family responsibilities is a coherence issue most working adults face constantly.

Some individuals usually avoid such conflicts through their ability to concentrate so fully on one goal that they make themselves forget that they also have conflicting goals. Making as many of your goals as you can into a coherent pattern can help you find a balance in your life.

Persistence in pursuing your goals can be a key to success. Are you initially excited by a goal, but do you quickly run out of commitment? Highly persistent people often refuse to change their goals. They keep plugging away until they get there.

Avoidance Justification is the opposite of persistence in goal setting. We decide a goal is unreasonable, and we justify avoiding it by either minimizing its importance or rejecting it altogether. This is not necessarily a poor response: Sometimes the effort truly is too great or the goal itself proves unworthy of pursuit.

Either persistence or avoidance justification can be appropriate in different circumstances. The difficulty arises when you rely overmuch on one or the other, turning yourself into a workaholic or a slacker.

Specificity and Measurability are important to goal setting, particularly important in job-related situations. How will you know when your goal is reached? The most successful weight loss programs encourage dieters to set a specific (but reasonable) goal: say 10 pounds, rather than just "I want to lose weight." Do you set a deadline for completion

Write three measurable, specific, clear and challenging goals for yourself. Write the same goals in ways that are not measurable, specific or clear. What is your difference in approach to the two sets of goals? Which set seems harder to accomplish? Which set creates a bigger charge?

If a high-jump coach tells athletes to jump as high as possible — without providing a bar to jump over — even the best can't accomplish much.

The effective approach is to put up a bar at a certain height, let the jumpers clear it, then gradually raise the expectation. The jumpers will rise to the challenge.

of a project or a specific phase of it? Or do you simply say, "I'll finish it as soon as I can"?

A key to good management is to let employees know exactly what's expected of them. Make the goals specific. Unfortunately, often we aren't nearly so specific with ourselves. The result is that we frequently don't accomplish what we could.

Degree of Difficulty is as important as measurability. Without a challenging goal you cannot expect to create a high level of charge. Indeed, if you know you can easily accomplish a task, your charge will be exceedingly low. This is a frequent theme of winning sports coaches who admit they set very high standards, knowing the high expectations will drive the players to meet them.

A real challenge will fire up your efforts. But this doesn't mean that you always should push yourself to the limits. Set too high a goal and after a time you may reject it as impossible. Your confidence will erode, and the charge created by goal setting will disappear.

Ideally, you should set reasonable goals that you have a good chance of reaching, but still remain challenging. This will create the charge that will allow you to accomplish your mission. Good managers recognize the effectiveness of challenging employees without setting goals so high that they are discouraged.

Students of habitual domains often ask me: "Should I set goals for myself which are well outside my habitual domain? Should my goals be at the edge of my HD? Or well inside my HD?"

The answer depends entirely on your degree of self-confidence. But a curious thing happens to ambitious people who set big challenges for themselves. Once they set a goal outside their HD, they find that goal becoming a part of their own habitual domain.

Generally speaking, setting very high goals is fine if you are able to view that goal realistically. You might set for yourself the goal of becoming President of the United States. Clearly, the odds against your becoming President are tremendous.

But as long as you realize how high that goal is, it's OK. You know you're probably not going to reach so lofty a position, but you still can take pleasure in the process of striving toward the goal. You may not succeed totally, but you will no doubt be enriched by the effort. On the other hand, no one is elected President *without* setting the goal to gain the office.

Time Horizons are useful in setting goals. Do you take a long-term or short-term view? Some of us can sacrifice short-term gains for long-term achievement. Others may prefer the enjoyment of short-term gains. Are you most comfortable with immediate goals or do you like to look ahead?

STATE EVALUATION

Are you **optimistic** or **pessimistic**? Do you generally see experience as favorable?

Do you evaluate situations by intuition or by **careful analysis** and **thinking**, or both? Where would you rate yourself on a 10-point scale on thinking or feeling?

Some of us go to extremes, but everyone exhibits elements of both qualities. Some gamblers may go almost exclusively on their gut feelings, while others are analytical players. In high stakes situations, they often rely on a combination. Mathematicians and scientists will usually rely heavily on thinking, especially in their research work, but there are times when nothing in research substitutes for the "hunch" that becomes a break-through hypothesis.

Businessmen rely on both thinking and feeling. A manager can look at an employee's work record, but cold, hard facts may not fully explain whether that person will be suitable for a particular job. The manager's intuition about and feelings toward the employee may be invaluable in making a decision. Some things just aren't quantifiable.

Generally speaking, **how long** does it take you to reach a clear-cut conclusion? Are you someone who reaches a conclusion, right or wrong, relatively quickly? Or do you hesitate frequently and delay making a decision?

Take a look at your **breadth** and **depth** of deliberation. Do you have difficulty in making judgments? If you're buying a mattress, do you read various consumer reports, compare prices and materials and visit several showrooms to test different products?

Or do you pick up the phone, call a department store and

List all your goals. Think about them as you list. Should you keep them written down for review? As you write them down, do you find yourself modifying them?

tell them to send over the best mattress for a certain price?

How much does **peer influence** affect you? Most of us are concerned about what others think of us.

Perhaps you're an individual who makes business decisions based entirely on your own internal agenda. You really don't care what others think of your conclusions.

At the same time, however, you may spend a great deal of time every morning choosing your clothing for the day. It's important to you that you present a certain image to your colleagues and customers. That's peer influence, too.

Once you've evaluated a situation, how *specific* are your conclusions? For example, "It will all work out in the end" is not a very clear statement.

But consider this alternative: "Things will work out fine because the worst that can happen under these circumstances is such-and-such. And I expect our outcome will be far less drastic than that."

How **stable** are your conclusions? Do you stick by them? Some people can take three days to come to a decision, and then they'll almost immediately change their minds. Salespeople call this buyers' remorse. It means the customers are second-guessing their own choices.

If you believe yourself to be a person who often makes mistakes, it will be difficult to commit to a conclusion. You lack confidence. The opposite of this is the rigid person who would rather die than change his mind, even though logically he may recognize a better alternative or course of action is available.

CHARGE STRUCTURES

A **high level** of charge is a necessary prelude to our tackling a task. Some people are easily moved to action. Others just don't get many high levels of charge. They're easygoing and unruffled about most events.

What are the main events that can cause a **change** in your charge structure? What changes your behavior? What raises your levels of hope or expectation? What excites you? Conversely, what upsets you, makes you angry or frightened?

Each of us responds to different sources creating different levels of charges at different times and in different circumstances.

Just about everyone will respond to a life-threatening situation. But only some of us will become infuriated when another driver cuts in front of us.

Remember: We're most sensitive to the events that create relatively high levels of charge. Monitor your emotions and compile a list of recurring situations that create a big charge in you.

The **distribution** of your charges dictates your ability to act upon them. At any given time you will have a number of high-level and low-level charges awaiting discharge. They are competing for your attention. Some lucky individuals have the ability to *focus* on one event or operation, temporarily ignoring all the other charges they carry.

Most of us, though, find it extremely difficult to function when we have too many charges. We concentrate best when there is only one event or problem carrying a high level of charge. Too many charges can keep you from focusing. In such a situation it is best to address those situations that are derailing your efforts. Get them out of the way, then concentrate on the most important job.

A persistent inability to focus suggests a problem that must be dealt with. Depression is one of the results of too many highly charged problems — particularly if the individual lacks the confidence and means to reduce the level of charge.

The **dynamics** of your charges affect their patterns over time. If you consistently have very low levels of charge you may be peaceful, calm and content, but you will almost certainly lack the urgency needed to achieve a specially targeted goal.

The extreme opposite isn't desirable either. Being continuously under a high level of charge can be exhausting and ultimately debilitating.

Ideally, we should be able now and then to empty out wishes and desires so that our level of charge is reduced (use the Deep and Down Principle). Meditation, prayer, simply enjoying nature can allow us to experience moments of calm. But when desired, we should let the charge build again, pushing us to action.

How do you *release* your charges? Ideally, you will have readily available solutions to your problems — skills and knowledge that can be applied to the problem — and you can turn a charge into positive action.

Swordmakers in bygone times observed that many potential buyers would run their thumbs along the blade of a sword in order to test its sharpness. These same individuals would usually neglect to examine the grip for defects. They failed to consider that a sharp blade on a bad grip would be no better — indeed, probably worse — than a mediocre blade.

All too often we examine only what is immediate to a problem, while ignoring the larger context. A common example: We often become so mindful of our career goals that we neglect family and health.

If you have no such available solutions, you must turn to either active problem solving (*i.e.*, looking for relevant information, testing possible responses) or avoidance justification (deciding the goal isn't as important as you once thought at this moment anyway).

Either approach — or a combination of the two — will reduce the level of charges. Both problem solving and avoidance justification are necessary for a healthy life. But too much problem solving creates too many charges; you become so busy you can't think effectively. And if you rely too much on avoidance justification, you'll never get anything done.

ATTENTION ALLOCATION

Each of us has 24 hours in a day. How we allocate this time to various events and problems tells us a lot about our behavior.

Try charting your activities over one 24-hour period. (See the form on page 191). You might be terrifically surprised at how you actually spend your time. I recall one student who after this exercise exclaimed, "I had no idea I spent so much time gossiping!"

How you spend your time makes up the **distribution** model of your attention allocation. How much time is spent on work? On socialization, on family? How much time do you put toward self-improvement?

Keeping a record of how you spend your day will provide an "attention map," a picture of your behavior. The actual time you devote to any particular pursuit is only half the story. The **quality** of attention to those events — their intensity coupled with their duration — can be just as important.

Important events will command intense and lengthy periods of attention; less significant items will have a milder, shorter duration.

Another way of examining quality is to look at the single-mindedness and focus you bring to bear on tasks. Some people can focus only for a few seconds and then their attention is drawn away. They simply cannot focus for long periods of time.

Instead of dealing with a task in one long session, they have found it more effective periodically to briefly shift their attention to other subjects, then return to the task at hand.

A student went to visit a wise master he hoped might become his teacher. The master invited the man for tea and began to talk with him. On every subject, the would-be student led the conversation, hardly allowing the master to speak.

Then, as they talked, the master began to pour tea into his visitor's cup. He poured until the cup was full; he kept pouring until the tea began to overflow. The visitor interrupted his own conversation to say, "Master, the tea is overflowing the cup!"

"Yes,' said the master. "The cup was full and I could pour no more into it. Just so, your mind is full and until it is emptied, there is no room for what I might teach you."

Who or what may be some of the sources for external information that are not tapped by most people? One rich source for experience is older people. It is their natural state to consult and they have much to teach, yet many times younger people reject them as old-fashioned. Consider taking advantage of some sources for information that others around you may overlook.

They've found it's easier for them to handle a big problem in several small sessions rather than one long one.

Planning is the key to many endeavors, particularly when it comes to business management. To what degree do you plan in advance your attention time allocation? Do you regularly map out your tasks, allocating time and intensity according to the difficulty of the goals?

Without planning, your time may be allocated by the urgency of arriving events. These are interruptions that can derail progress — a haphazard and highly ineffective way of achieving your goals.

INFORMATION INTERACTION WITH THE EXTERNAL WORLD

What are your **sources of information**? Do you go looking for input (solicited) or does most of it arrive unexpected (unsolicited)?

Is it from private **channels** (friends, co-workers, family) or from public sources (the media)? Which are your most important and useful sources? Which are trusted channels of information? Which don't you trust?

In obtaining information, what is your **degree of interaction**? How often do you actively seek external information? How much do you supply to others, and what channels do you use? How often do you keep things to yourself?

What are your preferred **information forms**? There are many possibilities: words, pictures, deeds.

If dealing with written or spoken language, which language? A foreign language, English or perhaps a highly technical language largely unknown to laypersons?

Another thing to consider is the way in which delivered information can be altered by the style of the person delivering it. Is the communication **straightforward** and **pointed**, or **tactful** and **diplomatic**?

Consider your favored **methods of information output**. Would you rather hold a conversation, write a memo, take notes? Would you prefer to say little while jumping to the task at hand? Are you tactful or blunt? Is your delivery still or animated?

TAKE TIME TO SMELL THE ROSES YOU PLANTED

A reminder: Once again, take your time. All this analysis can seem tedious or even impossible to do if you try to do it at one sitting.

Take one function at a time and consider it in a leisurely way. Let yourself explore your mind, your memories, your ways of interacting with the world. In effect, you will be mapping the landscape of your Self, your habitual domain. Everything you discover will be valuable and useful to you.

It's taken years to develop your Self. Don't try to complete this important exploration too quickly.

Challenging goals spur us to move actively in a direction we desire. Oliver Wendell Holmes, the great U.S. Supreme Court justice said, "The great thing in this world is not so much where we are, but in what direction we are moving."

跨過在您領域與外面世界的界線

Chapter 6

Crossing the Boundaries Between Your Domain and the World Outside

A ll of us become involved in myriad events (using the word event to also mean circumstances) which have a significant influence on us. To understand someone — ourselves or others — it's necessary to consider the events and problems that an individual deals with and how he or she handles them.

These circumstances or events can be domains in themselves (a company, for example, has a habitual domain). When they are part of our lives they also become part of our personal habitual domains. This is perhaps most obvious in the workplace. Next to home, no place is so familiar as where we work, and the people we work with can almost become a family for us.

Some events are simply that — an event or occurrence — such as moving from one city to another. But the effect of the event can have enormous impact on our habitual domains.

Given a habitual domain outside our own — for example, one's job — we can study it from the viewpoint of behavior functions: **goal setting, state evaluation, charge structures and attention allocation.**

We can also study it from the viewpoint of interaction

with others, as well as trying to understand the identification spheres and roles required by the external interaction.

These projections help us understand the details of the other habitual domains. They are also useful in examining the impact of the events, circumstances or other domains on our own decisions and behavior.

Habitual Domains and Events

The following are common events that affect just about everyone's life. It is impossible to understand your own habitual domain without taking such events into account.

Use these questions as checklists to think about yourself in relation to these "events."

PRIMARY JOBS AND JOB-RELATED ACTIVITIES

What is your contribution in your job? Who are your customers? (The customer here has a wider definition that includes your boss, subordinates, colleagues and the people to whom you provide service.) How much authority and responsibility does your position carry? Is the authority and responsibility clearly stated or implied? What are the reward and support systems? Are there opportunities for self-improvement, growth potential and advancement?

How do you relate to your colleagues, subordinates and supervisors? Does your boss provide opportunities? Do your colleagues support you? Are your subordinates loyal? How much time do you have to allocate to release charges created by your boss? How much do you participate in meetings, decision making, and information gathering, processing and assimilating? How much of your day is taken up with routine problems, fuzzy problems and challenging problems, and how do you handle them? Finally, what is the degree of satisfaction you derive from your job?

SOCIAL MISSIONS AND WORKS

What organizations do you personally identify with, from private clubs to international groups? What are your feelings of attachment to these organizations? What do you think is the ideal state for the organization? What is your degree of participation and identification with the group and its special projects? And, once again, what kind of satisfaction do you gain from participating?

HEALTH AND ILLNESS

How do you maintain your health? How much attention do you give self-improvement, exercise? Are you worried by illness? How serious are the illnesses? Can you accept them? Are you willing to let others know about your health issues?

EVENTS WITH INTIMATES

Intimate friends can be widely defined to include spouses, boyfriends, girlfriends, partners in business or friends with whom you share information about yourself. How much time do you spend with intimates? These relationships can create high levels of charge and strong memory and affect our performance in other situations.

FAMILY EVENTS AND PROBLEMS

How much time do you spend with your spouse? Children? What kinds of challenges does your family face? Examples include children's education, moving, health, adolescent problems, special events, parents' health, financial hardship.

However, it should be noted that the importance of this and other categories in forming one's habitual domain cannot be gauged simply on the basis of how much time each event takes out of your day. An argument with your spouse may take only a couple of minutes, but it can ruin your entire day.

HOBBIES AND SPECIAL INTERESTS

Hobbies or special interests could mean almost anything not job-related: watching TV, reading books, making art or music, athletic activities, cooking. The list is practically endless. What do you learn or get from having a hobby or special interest?

RELIGION, NATURE AND THE UNIVERSE

I'm referring here not to a narrow, dogmatic definition of religion but rather to spirituality in its broadest sense.

List the 10 activities you most enjoy. Does your life make time for you to do these things? If not, what is getting in the way? What can you change to allow yourself to do these things?

Every living thing is destined to die. Recognizing this directs our consciousness to a higher plane.

Every individual, whether a beggar or the head of a huge industry, is destined to die. Sooner or later each of us will, to some degree, take note of the origin and transitory nature of our lives. When I refer to spirituality I mean anything that takes us out of the linear, problem-solving thinking that dominates our day-to-day existence and directs our consciousness to a higher plane. This may include, but certainly is not limited to, organized religion.

The fact is that many of us spend more time every day contemplating spiritual matters than we realize. Among these moments we would most certainly include prayer and meditation. But also important is any undertaking that allows us to consider our place in the huge continuum of creation.

This might include our dream lives, or the act of quietly observing a work of art, or concentrating on the natural world. Watching and listening to a snowfall, closing one's eyes and listening to the sounds of wind and birds — these pastimes take us out of our usual problem-solving mode and move us to a higher dimension, an awareness of the fullness of our being.

Once again, the value of developing one's spirituality extends far beyond the actual time devoted to it. Persons who meditate for 20 minutes a day may decide that it's the most important, beneficial 20 minutes of their day, far outweighing any other pastime they could engage in. Do you take the time to explore your own spirituality?

Habitual Domains and External Interactions

Humans cannot live alone. They continuously interact with the external world to realize their existence and life goals. Thus their identification with and attitude toward the external world will have a great impact on their behaviors.

We will examine these ***external interactions*** in three areas:
- Identification spheres
- Role maps
- Attitude toward the external world

Identification Spheres

Identification spheres are the dimensions of connection between creatures. Examples of identification spheres in operation are easily drawn from the animal world where we see families, packs, herds and other identification spheres created by blood or instinct.

A jungle tiger will attack other animals but will identify strongly with and fiercely protect its own babies. The pet dog identifies more strongly with its pups than with its human masters. Mountain gorillas set themselves apart from gray gorillas.

Wittingly or otherwise, we constantly define the relationships among ourselves and external living objects, including people and organizations. For each living object, under different situations we consciously or unconsciously determine the desirability of its association and affiliation. For instance, sports fans who normally identify with only one college team will band together to cheer for the country's olympic squad, because their sphere of identification has shifted.

This determination can be instantaneous. When it is desirable to associate or affiliate with another person, organization or object, that object abstractly becomes a part of ourselves and we tend to work for or share the glory and dismay of the object's successes and failures.

When this happens I say we "identify with the objects under the specified situations." In such a situation, the collection of objects that we identify with is called our **identification sphere.**

Consider these common examples of identification spheres:

- If you have a favorite sports team, you're already part of an identification sphere, along with all the other fans of the team. You may not know these other individuals personally, but by virtue of your support of the team, you are part of a unit.
- Imagine you're traveling in a foreign country where English is seldom spoken. Walking through the town square you suddenly hear two persons conversing in English. You

Remember the people you admired when you were a child and the ones you wanted to be like when you grew up. How did they affect who you are and how you behave today? How did they influence your HD? Are they still good models for your life?

may introduce yourself to them. You have created an identification sphere based on your shared language.

If these individuals are also from America, then your sphere is that much stronger. If they actually come from your home state, then you've really achieved strong identification.

Identification is a natural phenomenon. Through analogy and association, we become identified with symbols. The "Star-Spangled Banner" or your school fight song can be the focus for an identification sphere.

Finally, identification is a function of time and situations. Groups of individuals who normally share a degree of conflict — such as management and labor — may find themselves within the same identification sphere when it comes to fighting against foreign imports. But when it's time to renegotiate union contracts, management and labor will be in opposite camps.

A husband and wife or parents and children normally would be in the same identification sphere, but not when they are involved in a family dispute.

COMMITMENT

There are, of course, degrees of commitment to an identification sphere. We're more likely to view our family ties as stronger than those that bind us to a professional organization. On the other hand, some individuals identify so strongly with a religious group that their identification to family fades by comparison.

Those who share the same ideology and background can command a stronger identification than those of differing backgrounds. Individuals sharing the common consequence of an arriving crisis can have such a strong identification that they are willing to die together. In a fire, a parent will risk death to save children. A fighting unit facing a common enemy is one of the strongest identification spheres imaginable.

But be aware that some identification spheres are much more durable than others. Identification based on profit usually cannot last as long as that based on shared ideology. As situations change, a profitability alliance can crumble; a sphere based on a deeply held belief is more likely to endure. Ideology usually has strong roots.

Identification with others is often a function of time and circumstance. A special moment with friends can create a lasting bond.

CHANNELS OF CONNECTION

To study the identification phenomenon, we need to pay attention to the channels of connection in a variety of situations. Just because you and a colleague are involved in the same organization, company or social event, doesn't mean you will be of like mind. You may still differ widely in your goal-setting functions, your state evaluation and the ways you as individuals process information. You and this person may have very strong ties under certain circumstances, but be at odds in other situations.

The strongest identification sphere involves persons with identical goals, identical views, identical consequences. In such a situation these people will work in concert to reach common goals no matter what the situation.

Such associations are, of course, rare. They almost never occur by chance; generally there is some leader who has worked to create an ideal association.

STRENGTH OF IDENTIFICATION

We can summarize our ideas on identification spheres this way:

The strength of identification of one person to another (or a person to an organization) is the aggregate strength of connections over all channels, events and situations.

It is important to note that the strength of an event is closely related to the strength of the circuit patterns representing the events. A person who had an alcoholic parent, for example, will have strong circuit patterns regarding drunken behavior. That person's spouse will almost surely discover that getting drunk may be an event that calls out very strong reactions from the partner who had bad memories associated with alcohol.

We can plot our identification sphere for any number of situations by using a set of circles or ellipses. Begin by putting yourself in the innermost circle. After all, you identify more with yourself than with anything else.

By using a series of concentric circles or ellipses, you can place virtually any object in relation to yourself.

In the accompanying identification sphere, your family may be in the circle immediately surrounding your "self."

This makes sense. For most of us our loved ones provide our closest and most cherished relationships.

In the next circle are intimate friends. If you identify closer to your intimate friends than your family, then the circle next to yourself would be your intimate friends instead of your family. Then, still moving out, we come to a circle that represents colleagues and co-workers. Finally we come to all living things.

From looking at this map we can see quickly where our loyalties and sense of identity lie.

You could make a similar map of your workplace. You would be in the innermost circle, surrounded by the members of your department. The next circle might include other members of the division in which you work. Beyond that is everyone working at the same factory or in the same office as you. Beyond that is the company as a whole, and beyond that, possibly, the parent corporation which controls the company you work for, as well as many others.

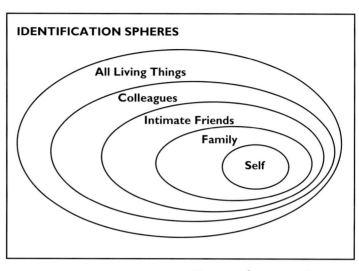

Everyone has connections to other living things. In most people these connections form identification spheres that relate to the self in this order, but others may find that friends are more closely connected than family.

MULTIPLE IDENTIFICATION SPHERES

Of course, identification spheres overlap all the time. Let's consider the intersection of two such hypothetical spheres. One sphere is based on religion.

It begins with yourself, of course, and then goes on to include other members of your faith, say as an example, Roman Catholics. The next circle out includes non-Catholic Christians. Beyond that are members of the Jewish faith. Moving yet further away, we find members of all non-Judeo-Christian faiths. Finally, farthest away from you, are non-religious individuals.

Now let's look at the second sphere, which is based on political outlook. Again, you are at the center. Let's say you are a political conservative. In that case, persons with similarly

Select some familiar or important situations, your job, family events or social activities, and begin to draw your identification and disidentification sphere. You'll begin to discover and become more aware of your HD, which is an important step to your self-discovery and expanding your HD. How about the identification and disidentification spheres of the people of importance to you?

conservative views will inhabit the next circle. In the circle beyond that are persons with moderate political views. And finally, as far away from yourself as possible, come liberals.

Please note that while in religious matters you identify most strongly with your fellow Catholics, in the overall scheme of things you identify more strongly with Catholics who hold conservative views like yours. You still have some identification with Catholic moderates, and a bit less with Catholic liberals. But you have virtually nothing in common with non-religious liberals.

Each of us has dozens of identification spheres relating to our place of employment, our living situations, our social and economic status, our education, religion, political beliefs, nationality, language and other concerns. All of them are continuously intersecting.

Such identification maps can help you understand yourself and others and how you perceive and interact with the external world. There are, of course, limits. A 100 percent accurate map of your identification spheres is impossible. But you can achieve a fair degree of accuracy if you are as objective as possible.

MULTIPLE DISIDENTIFICATION SPHERES

Before we move on, note that just as we can create an identification sphere, we can draw its negative counterpoint, a **disidentification sphere**. It is constructed in reverse order of the identification sphere — you are in the outermost circle, while those things you identify with *least* (or which you hate or fear) are at the center.

Sometimes, to get a handle on where our true loyalties lie, it is necessary to draw both positive and negative maps. For example, you may find that some of your colleagues at work can be identified as friends under certain circumstances, and those same persons may be viewed as adversaries under others.

Role Maps

All living things perceive their roles in life situations and act accordingly. When a strong male deer assumes the role of dominant buck, he will fight desperately against other males that move in on his harem of does. The doe assumes her role in perpetuating the species by waiting without interruption until the suitors fight and a winner emerges. But that same doe is capable of facing down a predator in order to protect her young.

Humans also assume different roles in different situations. Under normal circumstances the chairperson or CEO of a large company doesn't perform the job of a secretary. He or she will give orders instead of taking them. In an emerging company, however, an entrepreneurial president may take on many roles from making decisions to sorting the mail.

Understanding the roles we play is vitally important because by defining our roles we also define our possible actions. Our perceptions of the roles played by ourselves and others will vary over time and in different circumstances, yet they can also be stabilized so that a role becomes more or less permanent.

OFFICIAL AND IMPLICIT ROLES

First, examine the difference between *official roles* and *implicit roles*.

By taking an official role, an individual assumes the responsibilities, authority and power of that role. Among these official roles are president, director, manager, crew member, technician, salesman, receptionist, secretary.

Implicit roles are a bit trickier. Say, for example, that while driving down the street you witness a traffic accident and get out of your car to tend to an injured person. Officially you have no responsibility here. You're not a policeman or a paramedic. Yet you implicitly assume the role of policeman or paramedic — at least until the real thing arrives on the scene.

Here's an even more complex situation. Many informal groups or organizations have no clear-cut organizational

chart. Nevertheless, there always emerges a leader who motivates the others, who calls meetings or speaks for the group. That's an implicit role.

INSIDER AND OUTSIDER ROLES

In addition, we play **insider and outsider roles**. If you're one of the insiders in a particular situation, you'll have access to information, discussion and the decision-making process. You're part of the group that makes a final determination and takes the consequences.

The outsiders feel they have no particular reason for becoming involved in the process and generally do not intrude.

Most of us play both insider and outsider roles. If you're an assembly-line worker, you may be part of the team representing your union at the negotiating table. Under these circumstances you're an insider.

But when it comes to planning company-wide policy, you're an outsider. Individuals in management will formulate the policy and be responsible for the results.

Insiders tend to be more active and participative, while outsiders are generally passive.

We must always be aware of the drawbacks of a rigid insider/outsider situation. Suppose the management of a company is considering new product lines. The assembly-line worker is probably an outsider in these discussions. Yet it's entirely possible that he or she may have a useful insight into the problem, not to mention a vested interest. It's the worker's company, too, and its continued success will have a major impact on his or her life.

Therefore, good management allows for a relaxing of insider/outsider lines (it could be something as simple as installing a suggestion box or inviting employees to participate in group discussions). This will give employees an opportunity to switch back and forth between insider/outsider status.

SUPERIOR, EQUAL AND INFERIOR ROLES

Somewhat similar to the insider/outsider situation is the question of **superior, equal and inferior roles**.

Individuals who assume the superior's role tend to be domi-

With role maps we can see the myriad roles we play in different circumstances. Which of your roles are official or implicit? Are you sometimes an insider or an outsider? In which roles are you superior, equal or inferior? How easy is it for you to switch back and forth? What are the relationships between your different roles?

Our perceptions of the roles we play are grounded in childhood experiences.

nant, protective, independent, motivating and direction-setting.

Persons who assume equal roles will be independent, neither dominating nor submissive, less reluctant to express their views and willing to give and take based on reasoning and self-interest.

Those taking the inferior role will probably be submissive, dependent, passive and more willing to take orders.

Even within insider and outsider groups you will find superior, equal and inferior roles — in other words, a pecking order. As is almost always the case within organizations, a single individual may play any one of these roles in a particular situation.

And one must be wary of extremes. The individual who always assumes the inferior role will accomplish little. The person who thinks he's superior in all situations has a dangerous bias and will be an unfit leader.

TEACHER AND STUDENT ROLES

Two other roles we all play from time to time are those of **teacher and student**. When we believe we know more than others and have something to offer them, we become teachers. These individuals are protective, nurturing and expressive. Assuming the student role, we have a tendency to be polite, open-minded and willing to learn.

While playing the teacher may satisfy our egos, it's the student who receives the practical benefits and protection of this education. Good teachers invariably allow themselves to be students on occasion, providing their students with an opportunity to speak out.

As the song by Rodgers and Hammerstein so succinctly puts it: "If you would be a teacher, by your students you'll be taught."

PRINCIPAL PLAYER, CHEERLEADER, REPRESENTATIVE, MEDIATOR, AND ARBITRATOR ROLES

There are many other roles we may play in a competitive situation. Among them are those of **Principal Player, Cheerleader, Representative, Mediator, and Arbitrator.**

Each of these roles has explicit and implicit functions which we assume.

- Principal players assume the role of actually playing the game, whether on the sports field or in the board room.
- Cheerleaders work to instill the morale and spirit needed for the players to win.
- Representatives get behind one particular viewpoint.
- Mediators try to bridge the gap between disputing parties.
- Arbitrators hear both sides of a dispute and reach a fair decision for a settlement.

In the real world these roles aren't independent. One may simultaneously assume several roles and perform a combination of functions. Players taken out of the game become cheerleaders for their teammates. Most of us, though, have a habitual tendency or preference for playing a particular role or combination of roles.

Consider some familiar situations, your job, family, events or social encounters and map the roles you play according to the above description. This will help lead you to discover yourself better. How about the role maps of people of importance to you?

Attitudes Toward the External World

Finally we must take a look at our **attitudes toward the external world**.

Are you an **extrovert** or an **introvert**? The basic difference is that the extrovert likes interaction with the outside world and identifies through this interaction. In most circumstances this person will be outwardly directed.

The introvert tends to focus on himself or herself.

As is so often the case in examining the habitual domain, we find most people have elements of both the introvert and extrovert. Going too far in either direction leads to ineffectiveness.

For example, while the extrovert places emphasis on interactions with others, if that interaction consists of idle gossip, little will be accomplished. An extreme extrovert may be so eager for companionship that he or she never gets anything done.

An introvert is more likely to come to a decision by himself, but at the risk of obtaining insufficient information upon which to make that decision.

Are you more of an introvert or extrovert? To what extent do you use intuition and its opposite, analysis? How do these factors affect the way you perceive information? What benefits could you realize if you strengthened the factors of perception that you may not use much now?

Another distinction may be made between **self-oriented** and **externally oriented judgments**.

Self-oriented people tend to focus on those standards or assumptions that are applicable to themselves; externally oriented individuals focus on those applicable to external situations.

Self-oriented individuals may come to a conclusion quickly but miss the point; externally oriented people may reach a conclusion that is more accurate, but it often takes them a very long time to get there.

The most important factor may not be whether you are self-oriented or externally oriented, but whether you feel you have the competence in a situation to make a decision. Highly competent and confident individuals of either persuasion should generally perform well.

Does your identification tend to be **exclusive** or **inclusive**?

No doubt you've heard someone say, "If you're not with me, you're against me."

It's a perfect example of exclusive thinking. People who have this view regard everything outside of their identification sphere as part of the disidentification sphere. If you're not their friend, then you must be their enemy. Clearly this can be destructive, since it labels as enemies those who may wish you no ill will.

Exclusive types are usually closed, reserved, introverted and very careful in dealing with the unknown. Chances are they will view outsiders as potential enemies and treat them with suspicion and, in extreme cases, even cruelty.

Inclusive thinkers regard everything outside their disidentification sphere as a potential part of their identification sphere. They are more open, extroverted, expansive and possibly less cautious in dealing with outsiders. Since they regard outsiders as having the same nature as themselves, they tend to treat these outsiders with kindness and sincerity.

People are good hearted and decent. But this, too, is a dangerous assumption. Can you really be sure that outsiders don't pose a threat to you?

You'll note in our discussion of the elements that make up our habitual domains that most of us play various roles at different times. But inclusive and exclusive attitudes seem to be more enduring and unchanging than most of the characteristics we have examined.

Individuals tend to be predominantly inclusive or exclusive, with little variation.

Closely related are the **law and order** attitude and its opposite, a state of **flexibility**. Certain individuals emphasize strict adherence to the rules of those who share their identification sphere. In the absence of such obedience, these persons are frustrated and uncomfortable.

A flexible personality, though, emphasizes individual freedom and flexible relationships among the members of its identification sphere. They are uneasy with strict rules and procedures.

Inclinations toward **superiority** and **dominance** are instinctively connected to our life goals of survival, feelings of self-importance and social approval and respect.

However, feelings of **fairness** and **equity** among the members of an identification sphere suggest a more refined concept of social order; they are generally learned rather than instinctive.

Based on these two dimensions, people may be classified into four groups:

- *High equity and high superiority focus*: These individuals work on fairness and equity at the same time that they focus on their own goals of superior status. Grass roots political leaders in a democratic society are usually good examples.
- *High equity and low superiority*: They work hard on fairness and equity and de-emphasize the importance of superiority and dominance. Judges and priests are good examples of this group.
- *High superiority and low equity*: They push for superiority and dismiss equity as useless. Authoritarian leaders are good examples.
- *Low superiority and low equity*: These individuals have no interest in achieving superiority *or* equity. They may reach a state of self-actualization in which they detach themselves both from the desires of superiority and the disputes and discussions inevitable with equity.

Sun Tzu on War (and Business)

In his famous book The Art of War, *the ancient Chinese military strategist Sun Tzu stressed the need for a commander to know both himself and his enemy.*

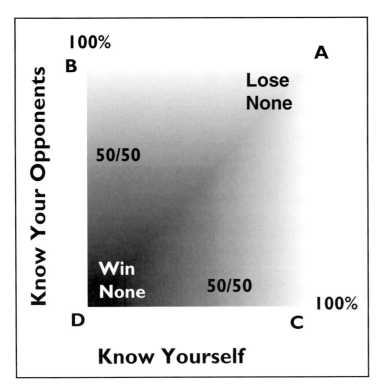

Though formulated as a guide to waging war, Sun Tzu's views can be easily paraphrased to apply to habitual domains and today's business world: If you understand your own and your enemy's habitual domain, you cannot lose in any battle. You might fight to a draw, but you cannot lose. This position is represented by point A in the accompanying graphic.

If you only understand your own HD but not your enemy's (or, conversely, understand your enemy's but not your own), your chances of winning or losing are 50-50 (points C and B).

If you understand neither your own nor your enemy's habitual domain, you can never win. Again, you might fight to a draw, but you cannot hope to win (point D).

Words and **deeds** are two key components to interaction among individuals. Some of us deliver more than what we promise, and some, much less. Some show their feelings through actions, some through words.

Some tend to overinflate their abilities, others to underestimate their abilities. Some easily accept requests but cannot deliver as requested; others accept requests only with a great deal of care and make sure to deliver on each request.

When misfortune strikes or failure occurs, some of us are prone to self-examination. We tend to assume **responsibility** for the failure and seldom blame others. In the same situation, others express **criticism**, finding fault with others and seldom blaming themselves. While few of us enjoy being criticized, some of us are able to take it positively; others cannot.

But there's more to these two concepts.

Young children don't understand what responsibility means. As they grow older, they realize what responsibility entails, although they often will try to avoid it. Most of us begin acting responsibly during our teenage years (or at least, exhibit selective responsibility). By the time we're old enough to move away from home, our sense of responsibility is pronounced.

Of course, some people continue to avoid responsibility throughout their lives. These individuals often find themselves trapped in a vicious cycle: They don't want responsibility, and others sense this. If there's a job to do, others perceive that the individual won't get it done and so don't assign it to the "irresponsible person," who then nurses feelings of resentment and disappointment, and the cycle continues.

When I talk to corporate executives I find that those on the fast track are always eager to assume new responsibilities. They see responsibility as an avenue to more money, more power, more promotions, more success.

Criticism also has additional layers. Those on the receiving end of criticism can react in several ways. They can ignore it altogether, giving the impression that it does not matter what anyone else thinks. They can take it too seriously, and end up nursing a grudge. Both of these are negative responses to criticism.

Or, they can accept the criticism exactly for what it's worth, taking it as seriously as it deserves. Sometimes criticism is considered and valuable. But sometimes you may recognize that the individual criticizing you is doing it just to be criticizing someone. Accepting criticism and recognizing its motive are positive responses.

As our HDs are more fully developed, we may begin to develop *"forgiving"* operators (circuit patterns). Realizing we are not perfect, we can begin to forgive others and to forgive ourselves unconditionally, instead of harboring guilty feelings against ourselves or grudges against others' misconducts as we perceive them.

Gossip and Information Exchange

Finally we come to the last element in the assessment of a habitual domain: **gossip** and **information exchange**.

By gossip I don't necessarily mean slanderous material about others. Gossip in this sense means casual and enjoyable exchange of information, even though it may contribute nothing to your primary goals.

Gossip can be highly satisfying. It satisfies our need for curiosity and external information, while pumping up our feelings of self-importance because we believe (wrongly) that we are better informed because of our ability to spread information.

Through gossip you can widen your circle of acquaintances and enter the identification spheres of others (just as they enter yours).

Gossip's downside is that the more it is passed around, the less reliable the information becomes. As people put "dressing" on information they distort it and it becomes inaccurate and unreliable.

Still, many so enjoy gossip that they eagerly exchange even this "dressed" information. Others pay little attention to gossip and are reluctant even to exchange reliable "undressed" information.

"Dressed" information can refer to exaggerated or erroneous information, but it can have a wider meaning. Some persons, when exchanging information, choose their words very carefully. They may couch information in certain terms which

Consider some familiar or important situations, your job, family events or social activities, and describe the attitudes you think you employ in the situations according to the above description. This exercise will help you discover and become aware of your unwittingly hidden HD, which is a vital step to self-discovery and to enriching and expanding your HD. How about the attitudes of the people of importance to you?

they think will least offend you. They've "dressed" the information. It may have been softened, it may even be deceptive.

For a classic example of dressed information, look at almost any example of advertising.

Other individuals may be brutally blunt in delivering information. Theirs is "undressed" information. A Marine drill sergeant's instruction to recruits may often be "undressed information."

What are the sources and channels through which you obtain your external information? Do you get your information from friends, peers, spouse, children? Formalized sources such as the media? Which channel, or source, do you rely on most? How do you process the information you get? How do you distribute information?

Understanding the way information comes to us is very important to our process of self-discovery. It is a key to seeing clearly how the world outside us affects our habitual domain.

Consider how solicited and unsolicited information affects you when you are making decisions. What effect do both kinds of information have when you are buying a car?

擴展你的習慣領域

Chapter 7

Expanding Your Habitual Domain

Once you have begun to assess and understand your habitual domain, you will see more and more the importance of expanding it. Like the reeds that bend and move in the flow of the rushing stream, flexibility will be your key to strength.

To be successful in any area of endeavor, you must be able to see life from a variety of perspectives. That's another way of saying that you have to broaden your habitual domain to include many ways of approaching experience.

The famed behavioral psychologist Abraham Maslow once noted, "If you only have a hammer, you see all problems as nails."

There's tremendous wisdom in that observation. Have you ever considered how engineers tend to cast every problem in engineering terms? That salespeople manage to turn virtually any kind of human interaction into a sales situation in which they make their pitch? That a clergyman views every problem as a matter of faith?

That's because we all have our own personal toolboxes with which to solve problems, and for most of us the number of tools at our disposal is limited.

If you're equipped only with hammers, your first inclination will be to hammer away, even if another tool would do a better job.

On the other hand, a person with a large, flexible habitual domain has plenty of tools at his or her disposal.

Many times you push past the boundaries of your habitual domain without realizing it. You are responding to experience with growth and learning. The ability of the brain to do this without conscious direction is one of the sure signs that every one of us has so much more potential yet to be realized.

Sometimes your habitual domain is expanded even whether you like it or not. Difficult or negative experiences can be very important to growth. Ernest Hemingway's observation that "the world breaks everyone . . . and afterwards many are strong at the broken places" is another way of saying that adversity can build a bigger habitual domain, one that has more coping skills within it.

You don't have to wait for experience — welcome or unwelcome — to come to you, however. You can take positive steps to expand your habitual domain. The more conscious opportunity you make to reach beyond your ordinary limitations, the closer you come to being able to use the vast potential that is yours.

Eight Basic Methods for Expanding Habitual Domains

While there are myriad ways to expand your habitual domain, here are eight basic methods. Each can be extremely useful when used alone. Their power is only multiplied when you combine two or more.

Some of these methods may strike you as elementary. But by giving them names and making them part of your habitual domain, you activate them. You'll be aware of them as never before, and they will be close at hand to help you in your quest for personal growth and success.

LEARNING ACTIVELY
Virtually every thinking person on the planet uses this method, if only in the most rudimentary ways. Any time you

decide to add to your knowledge store, you are practicing active learning.

When you decide to try cooking a new dish and begin following a recipe out of a cookbook, you are practicing active learning. When you are considering investing in stocks or bonds and study investors' guides, you're engaged in active learning. When your child is sick and you read Dr. Spock, that's active learning, too.

What I'm talking about here, though, is a very specific method of self-improvement. This method reaches beyond learning small pieces of knowledge, like a new recipe, to learning how to change your life.

There are *four fundamental steps* to this kind of active learning:

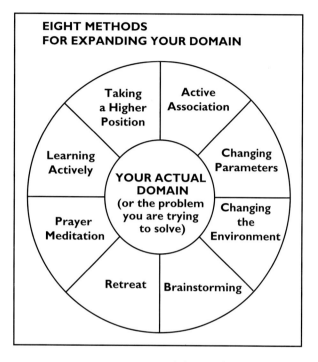

Any of these eight methods can be used to expand your actual domain. Often, more than one of the methods may be used at the same time.

• **Define your goal**. What would you like to accomplish if everything went your way?

That's a very big "if." Put away all your insecurities, shortcomings and fears and be honest with yourself. What would you really want if no limitations were placed upon you?

• **Identify those persons — past or present — who have achieved the goal you are striving for**. Has anyone done what you want to do or lived as you want to live? If you make a list, what are the traits these people have in common?

• **Study these role models**. If you aspire to the success of a certain historic individual, study his or her life as thoroughly as you can. If your role models are friends or colleagues, observe them. Get to know them. Watch how they behave in a variety of circumstances.

By doing so you will be building a circuit pattern, incorporating aspects of a role model's life into your own potential domain.

• **Use the models to help your decision making**. When

An Ideal Role Model

Identifying with an admired person can be extremely beneficial.

I once had a friend whose wife died, leaving him with two small children.

He remarried rather quickly and, putting his new wife in charge of the home, threw himself back into his career.

But things weren't going well on the home front. His new wife became increasingly moody and depressed. Before long she was spending entire days in their bedroom, completely ignoring the children, who were left to fend for themselves.

My friend was distraught and came to me to discuss the possibility of divorce. I listened to his story and, knowing that he was a devout Christian who had memorized entire chapters of the Bible, I asked him what he thought Jesus would do in this situation.

At first he was offended. "There's no comparison. Jesus is God, and I'm only a man."

"Of course," I said, "but imagine that Jesus had a wife who was behaving in this manner."

He thought for a long time before answering.

"Jesus would love his enemy, so he certainly would love his wife. I've got to pay more attention to her, show her that I really care for her."

In fact, his wife was so moved by my friend's change of attitude that she opened up to him about what was going on in her mind.

At the same time that she had taken on the burden of two children who weren't her own, her husband had become less and less attentive because of his job. She feared that he had married her only to have a full-time sitter for his children. His inattentiveness over the last few months had only reinforced her fears.

I'm pleased to report that several years have passed and that the couple remain happily married.

The key to this story lies with my question, "What would Jesus do in this situation?" Because of his devotion to his religion, my friend had built up incredibly strong circuit patterns reflecting his love of Jesus and his sense of just who Jesus was. Those circuit patterns were only waiting to be activated to create a model for my friend's behavior.

you are faced with a challenge, ask yourself this: If I were my role model, what would my role model do in this situation?

You'll find that those circuit patterns you have established in your potential domain will emerge in your actual domain, helping you to think like that person.

Suppose you want your child to grow up to have the attributes of bravery, decency and compassion. You could lecture day and night on these virtues, but you'd probably be tuned out at a certain point.

Here's another way. Give your son or daughter a biography of a person whom you regard as a role model in this regard — say, whomever you admire. It could be a sports figure such as tennis greats Arthur Ashe or Martina Navratilova, or a political leader, such as Mahatma Gandhi. Once your child reads the biography it will be forever a part of his or her potential domain.

True, he or she may consciously remember only certain facts about the person's life, but everything will be retained somewhere in the brain and will exert a subtle but steady influence.

Selecting a role model on which to base your own life is a common characteristic of highly successful individuals. You may recall that during the 1992 presidential campaign Bill Clinton made much of his study of Harry Truman. Whether you think Bill Clinton is in the same league with Harry Truman is immaterial. The fact is that Clinton's fascination with that earlier president could not help but incorporate elements of Truman's philosophy and personality into Bill Clinton's habitual domain.

Did it work? Well, like Harry Truman, Clinton scored an unexpected victory.

Here's another key point to be made regarding active learning: It only works if you're sincere, humble and attentive. Active learning is far less effective if you enter into it with an attitude of superiority. If you're going to learn, you have to assume the attributes of a dedicated student. Treat those who are teaching you with respect and appreciation.

To engage in active learning:
- *define your goal*
- *identify some persons who have achieved a similar goal*
- *study these role models*
- *use the models for decision making*

Look at it From the Boss's Point of View

A former student of mine was doing very well as the sales manager for an electronics company. But he became worried when his boss asked him to switch to a position in which he would be in charge of both personnel and purchasing.

"I'm good at sales, but I really don't know anything about personnel and purchasing," he said. "I'm afraid my boss doesn't like me and he's putting me into a job where he thinks I'll fail. That way he'll have an excuse for getting rid of me."

I asked him to pretend he was his boss and then examine the situation.

Suppose the boss really did want to get rid of him. Could he actually be hoping for a collapse of the personnel and purchasing departments just so he'd have an excuse to get rid of my friend?

My former student had to admit it sounded unlikely.

"But why would he put me in this job for which I have little preparation?" he wondered. "Unless, of course, he thinks I'm so competent that I can quickly learn the ropes."

Indeed, by thinking a bit more about it, my friend realized that if he could make a mark in personnel and purchasing, he would have competence in three important departments. That could only make him a more valuable employee.

In fact, maybe his boss was actually grooming him for an even bigger, company-wide job.

Now pumped up with enthusiasm, the fellow set out to learn all he could about personnel and purchasing. He was determined to do a terrific job.

He did. Now he's a vice president of the firm.

TAKE THE HIGHER POSITION

There's a tendency in all of us to view the world from a very limited, even selfish perspective.

"What's in it for me?" is often the first question from our mouths when faced with a new situation or opportunity.

Similarly, when faced with a problem we tend to look for the answer which is closest to home and probably easiest for us to employ.

There's a truism here: Given a system, we tend to look for the best solution within that system and pay minimal attention to other systems.

All too often, that attitude is limiting and self-defeating.

The failure of Communism largely can be attributed to the fact that Communist countries refused to look outside their planned economies to the benefits of competition and the free market system. They were so stuck inside their own system that they refused to consider any others.

In other words, the Communist leaders refused to take the highest position from which to observe things. The higher position in this case would have been to examine both planned economies and free market systems.

If your sales department is feuding with the production department, you could waste lots of time and energy arguing from your own self-interested perspectives.

But how would the company president view this situation? Taking the president's vantage point, you're forced to consider a larger range of needs and objectives. The overall health of the company is more important than the squabbling of two departments. You'll get a clearer picture the further you place yourself from lower-level pettiness.

By taking the higher position you are, in fact, expanding your habitual domain.

Many progressive companies *rotate* their potential executives so that they have an opportunity to work in each of the firm's departments. That way they will have a higher, more comprehensive view of the corporation.

Similarly, medical interns are required to rotate through various specialties — from pathology to pediatrics to plastic surgery — so that they will have the most well-rounded view of the care and treatment of the human body.

ACTIVE ASSOCIATION

Make a habit of looking for connections between seemingly disparate objects and events.

Here's an exercise. Find the common properties of the four following beings:

- A queen
- A professor
- A puppy
- A barber

Well, they're all living, organic beings. They're all mammals. They all must eat, drink and breathe. That's just for starters.

Ask yourself other questions. Which of the above would you rather spend time with, and why?

You can break things down further. Take the professor and the barber. What do they have in common? Well, they both provide services.

What about the queen and the professor. What do they have in common? Perhaps that within their own environments, they may give lots of orders and cultivate an aura of superiority.

What's the value of this? When you are comparing queens and puppies, for fun, ask which one you like better. The answer may reveal to you the secret of making people like you: Be loyal. This kind of association may just be the value of the mental exercise. But it is enormously important in research, in complex decision making, and in other areas where many seemingly disparate elements must be considered in trying to make sense of a situation.

Here's a practical example of active association being applied to a scientific problem.

For many years scientists had wanted to see the shape of atoms. Despite the development of highly sophisticated electron microscopes, their goal eluded them. We simply cannot "see" atoms.

Now in our everyday world we cannot only see objects, we can touch them. And that bit of active association gave the scientists an idea: Would it be possible to "feel" the atoms?

Eventually they designed an instrument that would use a laser beam to "touch" atoms and then draw the results of this scanning process through data fed into a computer. It worked.

CHANGING THE RELATIVE PARAMETER

Every event or problem has a number of parameters or characteristic elements. By tinkering with these parameters, changing their values, we can produce new concepts and ideas.

Imagine increasing your body size tenfold. If you did that eight times, your height would be greater than the earth's diameter. With your body that huge, your perception of our planet would be radically different than previously.

On the other hand, if you could reduce your body to one-tenth its size and do so consecutively eight more times, you would be so small you could hide in a single body cell.

In the business arena, you will find that if you are willing to change the parameters of a situation, you can generate new perceptions that will lead to better decisions.

An example: A company with only 10 employees would have a different management system than one with 100 or 1,000 employees. With the change in number of employees comes a need for change in management systems.

You can change your **personal parameters** too, sometimes by simply changing your expectations of yourself in a situation. Do you not have enough time for everything you do in a day? What if you got up one hour earlier? Changing that parameter would add seven hours a week, almost a whole working day, to your schedule. What if you cut out one thing you usually require of yourself? How much time could you gain to be used for other things you might want to do?

Water and fire are useful only when they lie in a reasonable range of "quantity." Gentle rain is romantic when you share one umbrella with someone you love. Rain that falls steadily enough to flood is terrible — the volume of water changes the parameter. Fire in a fireplace on a wintry night is cozy. Fire that consumes your house is a disaster.

CHANGING THE ENVIRONMENT

A change in environment is an extremely effective method for expanding your habitual domain. The new environment will provide new information to be absorbed by your habitual domain as it expands and adapts to the new situation.

There are several basic ways of changing your environment:

- **Move**. If you live in different locales you will, of course, be exposed to new situations and information. Even a small move can make a curiously big difference. What if you face your desk a different direction? What will you see every day? What if you change your usual routes, driving to your most familiar destinations along different streets? What will you see? What will these sights teach you or cause you to think?
- **Travel**. Different environments give us different stimuli. It's an old saying: "Travel broadens." These trips don't have to be to exotic lands. A Sunday drive to a nearby town can be a refreshing journey.
- **Go against your grain**. If you're a Christian, you can expand your domain by reading about Buddhism or Islam or any other religious or philosophical system. If you love rock and roll, listen to an opera.

This doesn't mean you have to agree with everything you encounter in your studies or your journeys. But that information will nevertheless become part of your habitual domain.

An admonition: To truly listen or study or read, you've got to adopt the state — the habitual domain, if you will — of the speaker or author you're concentrating on. If you can combine and reorganize all this incoming data with what you already possess, your habitual domain will widen beyond that of most other people. As a result, you'll come up with more and better ideas than others.

Businesses can effectively use changing the environment to stimulate growth. Some methods are:

- **Open a new market**. This is a perennial environment-changing move within the business community. Opening a new market can usually stimulate a company's growth.
- **Rotate managers and employees**. This is another classic business method. By gaining a familiarity with more than one department, employees and managers expand and enrich their habitual domains and the overall competence of the company.

When Sherlock Holmes wanted to solve some of his most difficult cases, did he go to his library or his favorite chair? No. He went to the theater to watch a play. He got away from the environment of his workplace. In a place where you will see it, leave yourself a note of five places you could go the next time you are looking for fresh ideas.

Tai Ghee

Tai Ghee means ultra-limit, in which there is no limit.

In Tai Ghee, you are one with the heaven and the earth, identifying yourself with everything and nothing!

In Tai Ghee, you empty yourself of all desires. You focus on the energy flow which is ever continuous and smooth in your body, which itself is a universe.

In Tai Ghee, you return to the God, the Creator. You are like a newborn babe, ever pure and beautiful, unpolluted by any socially acquired desires.

In Tai Ghee, you are pure, unprejudiced and non-judging. Your spirit is everywhere and nowhere. Everything is beautiful to you as it is unfolding.

BRAINSTORMING

Brainstorming is nothing more than effective group thinking. Presented with a particular problem, each member of the group is asked to freely report what comes to mind regarding various aspects of the situation. It can be an enormously creative process, not only to meet a challenge the group faces (such as increasing sales) but also to encourage individual growth. Good brainstorming sessions let everyone feel they are drawing upon the best creative potential.

The first step encourages different ideas to emerge and is called the **divergent** thinking phase. The ideas generated may be good or bad, but for the time being judgment should be suspended. There's no point in having the participants so fearful of criticism that they close their minds and fail to contribute.

The second step is the **convergent** integration phase. The group focuses on the ideas that have been presented. People associate concepts to find relationships among seemingly different ideas.

The objective is to arrive at a final solution satisfying to all. To be effective at this stage, the group must focus on its objectives and how the ideas generated can be applied to those goals.

Brainstorming only works in an atmosphere of mutual respect and trust. The leader of such a session must be tactful and perceptive in order to make every participant feel like a contributing member. Sometimes a good exercise is to have each member of the group write ideas on yellow sticky notes, one idea to a note, each idea related to a stated objective of the brainstorming session.

Everyone then sticks the appropriate notes under each objective — achieving a preliminary grouping, or convergent integration. These groups of notes can then be used to reach solutions.

RETREAT IN ORDER TO ADVANCE

Confronted with Wonderland, Alice lost her power to concentrate. It seemed to her that everything just got "curiouser and curiouser." That can happen to anyone who is trying to solve a problem, or push on to a higher level of learning.

When facing high-stakes situations, it's natural to feel uneasy. This is because we suddenly become aware of the limitations of our actual domain. With sufficient thought or awareness of possibilities, we may uncover a good example waiting in our potential domain.

An example from history:

The ancient Greek scientist Archimedes served the king of Syracuse. The king possessed a golden crown but was concerned about whether the crown was really made of pure gold.

He challenged Archimedes to prove the purity of the crown or to lose his position at court.

Archimedes brooded on this problem until one day he stepped into a full bath and saw the water flowing out. The result was his formulation of the displacement principle: the volume put into the water should be equal to the volume of water displaced.

Then Archimedes could solve his problem. He measured the volume of water displaced by the crown. He determined the weight of pure gold that displaced the same volume as the water displaced. Archimedes compared that weight to the weight of the crown. They were the same, and the crown was indeed made of pure gold.

Sometimes taking a time-out from the matter can be the most effective mind-expanding technique you can use.

- **Leave the problem temporarily**. When you're stuck, it's time to retreat. Leave things alone. Don't think about it.

  Actually, you're not admitting defeat. By backing off you increase your chance of solving the problem in the future.

  Since you have different thoughts at different times and in different situations, your actual domain and reachable domain can be quite different at different times. As you retreat you're activating different sets of ideas, and some of them may be just what you need to tackle your problem.

- **Take your time**. Good problem-solving strategies don't happen overnight. But if you keep facing a problem, you'll whittle away at it.

- **Dump your assumptions**. Every now and then—once a day if you can—try to rid yourself of all the assumptions you've built up. This gives you a fresh new outlook and provides new perspectives and solutions.

This method of retreat can also be used to improve your personal relationships. For instance, you may think that a co-worker is your enemy in the office. If you step back and convince yourself that he's actually an ally, your attitude toward him will change. It's even possible that with a change in your attitude, he will become your ally.

PRAYING OR MEDITATION

During a busy day you are almost certain to create high levels of charge. When that happens your mental focus is restricted and only those ideas and operators with strong circuit patterns can catch your attention. You're not able to bring the full powers of your habitual domain to bear on problems.

Some of the most effective ways to lower your overall charge are through prayer, meditation, relaxation exercises or through a conscious effort to put aside your unfulfilled wishes.

Of course, not everyone adheres to a religious faith or tradition. That's OK. It's not necessary to accept any dogma or religious credo in order to have a spiritual life. You can

Write your biggest problem or desire in the form of a question at the top of a blank piece of paper, says Brian Tracy in his great exercise for brainstorming. Come up with 20 answers to the question. Write down anything that comes in your head. When answers are slow in coming, consider the opposite to answers you have already listed. Do this every day for a week. Do it with different problems. In days, you can have more than a hundred approaches to questions that have bothered you for years. Put into practice only one or two of the ideas and you will be making progress you have never imagined before.

reach your spiritual dimension through appreciating nature, simply relaxing into the sense of a larger universe, beautiful in its proportions and vast scope.

Letting your mind find its spiritual realm is a way of releasing your charge, thus allowing good ideas to catch your attention.

The Bubble Necklace

Expanding your habitual domain does not mean you will get everything you want. But you will meet more goals than if you had kept yourself narrowly bounded. And you will understand and enjoy the whole process more.

Once, a child was fascinated by the bubbles floating on the surface of a stream.

"Make me a necklace of those pretty bubbles," she demanded of her father.

"Certainly," he replied. "I'll be more than happy to make you a necklace if you can pick up the bubbles and hand them to me."

When the child tried to grasp the bubbles, they burst. She was disappointed but delighted at the same time at the fragile bubbles, and at the little joke she saw that the father had played on her.

Sometimes when we can't approach a problem or meet a demand, we can offer an alternative that changes the situation. An expanded habitual domain makes this possible because we are able to see the situation from a different — and productive — perspective.

讓您的腦和手為為他工作

128

Chapter 8

Let Your Brain and Behavior Work for You

Some years ago a highly successful business-man saw his corporation collapse after a drop in stock prices. He was so depressed that he considered killing himself.

Fortunately, before he acted on this impulse, he called a good friend and expressed his unhappiness and self-destructive urges.

The friend listened sympathetically and then suggested, "Before you decide what to do, let's calculate exactly how much you've lost."

On a piece of paper the friend drew a vertical line. On one half of the page he wrote "assets" and on the other side "losses."

"Let's start with your assets," said the friend. "Are you married?"

"Of course. You know I'm married."

"Well then, is your wife faithful?"

"Certainly she is. Devoted to me, in fact."

The friend wrote down under assets: "Good and loving wife."

"Any children?"

"Yes, a son and a daughter."

"Have they been a great disappointment to you? Have they run away from home or gotten in trouble with the law or turned against you?"

"No." The friend listed as assets, "Son, daughter, both very fine young people."

"How about your health? Any heart problems?"

"No, at my last checkup the doctor said I was very fit."

The words "very healthy" were jotted down in the assets column.

"Would you sell your heart for $100,000?"

"Of course not."

"How about for $1 million?"

"No."

"How about $10 million?"

Several more similar questions were asked, and then the businessman interrupted his friend.

"OK, no more questions," he said. "I don't want to kill myself any more. It looks as though I have a great many valuable things in my life besides my company."

Observing this situation from the outside, you may conclude that the solution employed by the friend was pretty obvious. It was based on the old admonition to always look on the sunny side of things, to count your blessings.

But that's because you were on the outside. In the depressed businessman's position you, too, might have been tempted to destroy yourself.

Positive Restructuring of Your Actual Domain

Having an active and growing habitual domain does not mean that you will never fail. But it does mean that you will have the resources to come through it and start again with renewed energy and commitment.

Let's say you're very discouraged. What can you do about it? Actually there are a few very simple efforts that will reap big dividends.

Physical Movement can help you to control your confidence and mental power. Happy, self-assured individuals raise their heads, stick out their chests and straighten their backs. They don't consciously think about it — their posture is a reflection of their mental state.

When you're down, instead of succumbing to a slumping, defeatist posture, force yourself to move as though it's the best day of your life.

Instead of your emotions ruling your body, your body will send a message of confidence and satisfaction to your brain. You will indeed feel confident and satisfied.

Mental Focus is the power of attention allocation I have mentioned before, and it can quickly boost your energy and mood. If you put your mind — allocate your attention — to an elevating goal, and believe you can achieve it, the goal will create a charge, and resulting drive and action. Your mental power will be activated and brought to bear on achieving the goal.

Dwelling on your misfortune can be self-indulgent and self-defeating. Focus on a task or goal, personal or professional, and by visualizing that you have reached it you will raise your level of confidence. Goal setting lets you control the charge your brain is receiving.

If your unhappiness is the result of persistent destructive behavior on your part — say, overeating — use your mind to vividly imagine the bad consequences of this behavior over time: weight gain, clogged arteries, even early death. The more vivid the mental picture you paint, the stronger the charge you will feel to change your behavior.

State evaluation also helps to control your mood. Evaluate a situation realistically, but look for positive aspects. If you're walking through a dark tunnel, imagine there is a light at the end. This provides hope and gives you the impetus to keep walking. When facing a thorny problem, you can use the same imagination to instill hope and confidence.

State Evaluation gives you control of your expectations and increases your optimism. When you commit your mind to the expectation that you will be equal to a task, you most likely will be. "I can do this" is one of the most important things you can learn to say to yourself.

You can do it, if your mind and behavior work for you. Here are several important concepts that can be used to make that happen.

THE SELF CONCEPTS

In the core of your habitual domain, there are pervasive concepts about your **Self**, including your **Ideal**, your **Roles** and your **Self-love** or **Self-esteem.**

Your **Ideal** can be: What do you want to be? What's the ideal state of your life? What person would you like to model yourself after?

Think of two times in your life when you successfully talked yourself out of trouble.

Your **Roles** defined by yourself can be: What do you want to do in your life? In what role do you cast yourself in your job situation? In your family? In your community? In the grand scheme of things?

The third and most interesting concept about yourself is **Self-love**. Self-love isn't the same thing as selfishness. But if we cannot love and respect ourselves, we cannot hope to have those feelings for others.

One way to build Self-love and Self-esteem is to cast yourself as a role model. Parents often reject bad or questionable behavior because they want to set good examples for their children. Managers do not want to appear lazy; they want to set a good example for their employees.

Another way is simply to reinforce Self-love every day by talking to yourself. Looking into the mirror each morning, tell yourself:

"I love myself. I appreciate myself. I love and appreciate others as well. I'm grateful to the Creator for my blessings, and I'm grateful to other people for their support."

Usefulness and value can come in many forms.
Celebrate your differences.

Once you get comfortable with this basic conversation with your Self, you can move on to specific encouragement. Do you have an important presentation? Look yourself in the eye and say, "I am going to do a great job today." Need to feel your best? Look in the mirror and talk about yourself as if you were a stranger: "What a beautiful woman! She's wearing a terrific suit. She has such a pleasant face."

Perhaps you can't imagine yourself doing such a thing. You would feel silly. You may think this sounds like pop psychology or psychobabble.

Not at all. Scientifically speaking, this method works for the simple reason that it reinforces our already existing circuit patterns for love and appreciation.

If you want to pump up your biceps you go to the gym

and practice curling weights. You don't do it once and then quit. You do it every day, or as part of a regular schedule. Think of your biceps as a circuit pattern. With repeated exercise this muscle/circuit pattern gets stronger and stronger.

It works the same way with Self-respect and Self-love.

Most parents know how important it is to instill self-respect in their children. They can do this with encouragement and praise. Good managers know the benefits of congratulating employees on a job well done. Neither parents or managers really succeed unless they make an effort to say to the people they are encouraging, be it child or employee, "I am proud of you."

Unfortunately, we often tend to neglect Self-respect in ourselves. Very few people ever look themselves in the eye in the mirror and say, "Good job. I am proud of you." Try it. You'll be amazed how much it does for your Self concept.

THE EXPECTATION PRINCIPLE AND MENTAL LIGHT CONTROL

Expectations can be a tremendous motivational force. If you place **high expectations** upon people and give them encouragement, they will excel.

Note that there are two parts to this principle. First, high expectations or goals. And second, encouragement or confidence.

The Best Teachers

Three high school teachers were called to the principal's office and informed that since they had been judged to be among the best teachers in the school, they would be placed in charge of classes filled with the brightest students.

"I've no doubt that with your skills and the high level of intelligence among these students, that your classes will perform outstandingly," the principal told them.

At the end of the semester standardized tests were given, and the three teachers' students scored 20 percent to 30 percent higher than the class norm.

The principal congratulated the teachers on their outstanding efforts.

"Actually it was the kids," one of the teachers replied.

"They were so smart to begin with."

"I don't think so," said the principal. "You see, they weren't as gifted as I first indicated. In fact, they were chosen randomly from the student body."

The teachers were at first perplexed by this, then delighted.

"I guess we really are the best teachers you have," one said.

"Well, not really," the principal replied. "You three were chosen randomly as well."

Because the principal had given the teachers positive encouragement and high expectations in advance, they had high expectations of themselves and their students. This strengthened their determination and confidence that they could attain the goals they set out to achieve. Although the students were randomly chosen and not necessarily more intelligent than others, through the expectation and hard work of the teachers, they too excelled.

Expectation creates a charge; confidence turns the charge into drive force. Together they increase our ability to achieve a goal.

It happens all the time in everyday life when a parent tells a child: "You're really looking great in soccer practice. I bet you can score a goal in Saturday's game." Thus armed, the child is much better equipped to play well and possibly score a goal.

Of course, there is no guarantee that the child will have a great game. If not, is the whole effort a waste?

Hardly. In any effort, if you can enjoy each step in the process of improving, you will have gained much.

On the other hand, if each step toward your goal is painful and tiresome, you're unlikely to reach your destination. And even if you do, you may not be particularly pleased by your effort, which may then seem to have been too great for the reward.

Lighting Up Control is to set your mind on the positive side of possible results. Try to see and feel the consequences of success before you actually attain it. By changing your actual domain, you will generate yet more charge and increase the likelihood of actually reaching the goal.

Try to reward someone in your office or home with praise. Watch how they respond and how they may behave differently with you in the future. Can you use this technique effectively more often in your life?

Moreover, the pleasure of success is not limited to the end of your efforts. By anticipating success, you have a taste of it as you progress. There is much to be said for the old adage, "Look on the bright side."

It is important to believe that you will succeed. The belief creates a charge and keeps you focused on success and your chances of attaining it.

MENTAL FOCUS CONTROL

Mental Focus Control permits us to control the activation of circuit patterns in the brain to control our moods, judgment and behavior. Remember, you feel happy or sad because your actual domain (the circuit patterns presently activated in your brain) are happy or sad ones at the moment. If you can change your actual domains, your mood, related thoughts and behavior can be changed as well.

Instead of being the victims of our emotions, we can learn to change them to states we want. Suppose you're walking through a cemetery on a dark night. It's creepy. How do you prevent yourself from becoming afraid?

Try *singing*. It works because we have to employ our mind to recall the lyrics and melody, while employing our facial muscles and body to sing. These efforts activate our circuit patterns related to music. As our attention is occupied by these circuit patterns, we're too busy to be frightened.

In fact, music has tremendous power to change your mood. When you're feeling down, the tendency is to listen moody music that reflects your gloom.

Instead, play something upbeat, even funny. Your circuit patterns for lighthearted musical enjoyment will kick in.

Actually, your brain is the world's most comprehensive jukebox, only instead of just songs, it holds emotions. And with the punch of a mental button, you can call up those emotions and experience them. You can bring back the elation of crossing the finish line in a race run 30 years ago or recall the nervous anticipation of the first day of kindergarten or college.

Depending on which button you choose (where you put your attention), you can change or reinforce your mental attitudes and your mood.

Suppose you need to buck up your ***confidence***. Think

about a time when you felt incredibly self-assured and happy. Perhaps it was getting an A on a big exam, winning an important game, earning a major scholastic award, making a big sale or successfully completing a project. By recalling those memories you can relive those positive emotions and carry them over to your current life. Let the circuit pattern for success, confidence and happiness occupy your mind.

A key advantage of Mental Focus Control is the **ability to look at negative experiences in a new and positive light**. All of us will experience failure. The question to be asked of ourselves is, "What did I learn from this matter?"

The answers to this question can change the circuit patterns that are activated in our brain. We will be able to look at the event more positively and constructively. Our minds will give us better suggestions to solve the problem.

Mental Focus Control is a positive force, but it carries a **contrasting negative aspect**. Because you can focus sharply — that's what allows you to control your attention — you will always be leaving something out of focus as you think. Your mind is somewhat like the lens of a camera. When you focus your lens on an object and shoot, you will probably neglect everything outside the frame of the picture.

When you are observing experiences or the behavior of others, it is good to remember this. People can't get to know each other just by taking a glance at each other, or even by focusing on one aspect of a person just met. To take in enough information to form good judgments, you must shift your mental focus, considering different facets of a situation or another person.

When you are trying to change your emotional state or to make up your mind *to act* on a problem, your mental focus control needs to be exclusive, shutting out what's unwanted or unneeded at that moment. When you are trying **to expand your understanding or knowledge**, your mental focus needs to be inclusive, shifting to take in lots of new information.

To strengthen your Mental Focus Control, use some of the techniques I talked about in Chapters 4 and 7. Look for the positive side in whatever is frustrating you. Take the higher view. Or try thinking about your problem or dilemma from another angle, not positive or negative so much as simply different.

Here's an exercise to try that will show you exactly how the mind works in creating mental focus. Look around the room, making a special point to notice all the objects that are blue. Now close your eyes and recall all the objects you can that are red and what their shapes are. If you are like most people, you will not know where all the red objects are or be able to describe their shapes. The experiment tells us that if we choose to pay attention to blue, we will neglect much of the appearance of other colors.

Ask yourself encouraging questions. Don't say, "Why me?" or "Where did I go wrong?" Try, "What valuable insight will come to me from this experience?" or "What should I do to reach an agreement?" Positive questions trigger positive responses in your brain and you will feel more confident and resourceful.

BUILDING CONFIDENCE

Fear of failure, fear of success and *fear of rejection* can result in a lack of confidence. An athlete may want to win a competition and enjoy the prestige that goes along with it. But if he fears failure, he may not even try.

Or perhaps he fears that if he does win the medal, he will be expected to endure even more intense training, more competitions and increased pressures. In this case, he fears success, which can be just as debilitating.

An employee may desire a good relationship with his manager. But he may also fear that too much close contact will result in being asked to do extra work.

Fearing rejection, a salesperson may procrastinate in making necessary phone calls because she's afraid customers will turn her down. Or what about the lovesick individual who cannot manage to express passionate feelings for fear of rejection?

These fears usually have their *sources* in the following:

- Lack of clarity and consistency of goals. When goals are unclear, conflicts among them are inevitable. This results in uncertainty, indecisiveness, worry and fear. For example, the dual goals of good quality and low price simply may not be possible in some products.
- The dominance of negative circuit patterns regarding success, failure and rejection.

We can combat these by recalling successful experiences.

Or, we can put ourselves in the position of never failing by seeing that gaining experience constitutes success: "I cannot fail unless I don't learn anything from this situation."

We can redefine success to make it easier: "If I can learn something, or if I'm still trying, I'm successful." One reason we are afraid to take risks is that we define success too stringently.

Visualization is a method we can use to experience ideas because our brain doesn't differentiate how a circuit pattern was created, whether it was by real experience or visualization. Use visualization to nurture your learning process. Apply it to specific situations where you want to grow, perhaps in your work, or in a sport.

Knowledge of others is wisdom.
Knowledge of the self is enlightenment.
Mastery of others requires force.
Mastery of the self requires strength.
— Lao Tzu

The Sun's Lesson

Only one woman ruled as an empress in Chinese history. Her name was Wu Zer-Tian. During her reign, she developed many worthy ministers and raised her son to succeed her. But when she grew old, the ministers and her son could not wait for the throne and they conspired to overthrow her.

When the coup was successful and she was removed from power, the aged empress languished in her chamber. All day and night Wu Zer-Tian said to herself, "These are the people I helped. Why did they do this to me? What caused this traitorous behavior? Why are they so ungrateful?" She was consumed by this.

She was so miserable that she could not rest enough even to die. Finally she asked an enlightened monk for a solution.

"Do you see the sun which gives light and heat to everyone equally?" he said. "It doesn't distinguish between good people and bad people, giving more heat and light to the good and less to the bad."

From this lesson, the empress realized it was not her responsibility to judge her son and the ministers or right from wrong. Not even the great sun judges, she said to herself at last. It is not our obligation to judge.

According to legend she died happily with a smile on her face. Through acceptance, she had come to peace.

The comedian George Burns, then in his 90s, was once asked, "What is your definition of success?" He answered: "To keep on breathing."

You can also redefine rejection. Remind yourself that you are a priceless living entity. Just because one attempt at communication or one activity of yours is rejected by another, it doesn't mean that all of the myriad possibilities that make up your Self have been rejected. Many ways are still open to you to reach your goals.

Become an Observer of Yourself

It's an interesting paradox of human behavior that when something goes wrong in our lives, we often find it perversely pleasurable to dwell on our unhappiness, to chew it over again and again.

This can be a tremendously self-destructive trap that can sap your confidence and limit your growth. What's doubly ironic is that getting out of this situation is amazingly simple.

When you find yourself in this cycle of self-imposed misery, ask yourself *why* you're unhappy. It doesn't matter what the answer is. Just the process of posing the question lets you step outside your misery and become an observer/analyst, looking at your unhappiness.

Before you asked the question, you were a slave to feelings of unhappiness. With this incredibly easy method, you become an observer and gain a measure of control. You may think this is too easy to be true, that it's all semantics. But I assure you, it works.

On a 3-by-5 card, write down 10 strong and constructive self-suggestions that can empower you to become more powerful, positive, active and confident. Carry the card with you and use it to remind yourself of your potential.

習慣領域的解剖

Chapter 9

Anatomy of the Habitual Domain

ach of us has a habitual domain that is unique. Organizations of all kinds also have habitual domains, similar to individual domains in the way they can be understood, but, of course, different in some important aspects.

As you have read this book, you have probably begun to see that some elements of the concept of habitual domains appear in descriptions of human thought and behavior in various cultures. It may be expressed in different ways, but the core concept is the same. Each of us has a Self that is uniquely our own, but the Self can be expanded to take in new ideas, new information, new possibilities.

Each of us may develop a picture of our habitual domain, a way to think about it in concrete terms. Earlier, I said it was like a snail's shell, going with the snail everywhere throughout a lifetime. Another person might see the habitual domain as a house with all the hopes, memories, fears, dreams, and experiences of a lifetime serving as the "furniture" of the rooms; a quiet courtyard at the center of the house is a haven for meditation and rest, while beyond the doors the busy street offers a place to go to find new experiences. Someone else might see the habitual domain library which collects a large number of books registering a wealth of experiences, thought and judgments. Some books are frequently retrieved and used, while others are not.

We may each picture it differently, but my studies and reflection have led me to see that no matter how each of us imagines it, the habitual domain really has an anatomy, an essential structure that can be analyzed. That analysis has formed the basis for the self-discovery this book has been designed to lead you toward.

The ideas and operators that may be regarded as memory and "programs" are like a human "software" for the super-computer of your brain. This software can be reprogrammed and upgraded. The collection of ideas and operators is your habitual domain.

Let's review briefly to help you get the concept of habitual domains well within your own habitual domain. For individuals, the habitual domain is made up of four elements:

- **Potential domain**: all the ideas and operators that can potentially be activated in our brain.
- **Actual domain**: the ideas and operators that actually are being used at one time.
- **Activation probability**: the likelihood that particular ideas and operators will be activated.
- **Reachable domain**: new ideas and operators generated by the current or actual domain.

A Singing Star's Discovery

Some years ago a young singer on the eve of a big concert found he could not get the sleep he desperately needed because of the crying of a child in a nearby hotel room. The singer expected the child to exhaust itself with the loud bawling, but instead the cries became louder and continued for hours.

Fearful that he would be in terrible shape for the next day's performance, the singer became extremely annoyed and agitated. As his frustration mounted, though, an unexpected question came to his mind. How, he wondered, could this child not be tired after crying for so long?

144

The singer then began listening very carefully and found that the child actually was crying using a form of deep breath controlled by his diaphragm. Hence, the baby did not tire of making the sounds.

The singer decided to try this method, and he began practicing in earnest. In a relatively short time he had mastered the technique and was a rising star in the opera world.

His name was Luciano Pavarotti.

This story is a lesson in the importance of controlling one's actual domain. Had Pavarotti allowed his actual domain to remain in an anger state because of the child's crying, he would have learned nothing and spent his night in helpless frustration.

Instead he changed his actual domain to view the situation as a learning experience. The result of that decision is now celebrated throughout the world of music.

The **core** of your habitual domain is the set of ideas and operators that are most likely to be activated at any given moment. These are the important basics of your Self, put in place by your own talents and interests, your experiences, your interactions with others (especially parents and teachers when you are very young), and the knowledge base you have put in place with your studies, travels and conversations. Thus, the core includes your personal beliefs, your names and enduring habits.

Every part of your habitual domain can be changed — ideas, behavior, even your core set of ideas. Some changes, like adding a happy new experience to your memories, are easy. Other changes, like giving up a long-held belief or an ingrained habit, are difficult. But changes are possible because your brain is a supercomputer that can be continuously programmed and your human "software" upgraded. Your capacity to program learning and change is huge, almost unlimited.

From the beginning of human reasoning, people have understood that the great truths of life are usually not to be observed directly. Lao Tzu, a famous Chinese philosopher, said that we can only see Being on its Way by the results of

The Fast-Tracker's Husband

Once upon a time there was a young vice president of finance who was on the fast track. She worked long hours and often didn't leave the office until 7 or 8 at night. Even then she usually was carrying work to be completed at home. The fast-track vice president was under considerable pressure. Unfortunately, when she needed to vent, the target usually was her husband. She spoke rudely to him and often criticized him.

He didn't appreciate this and reciprocated in kind. The marriage soon deteriorated into an uneasy and frustrating relationship marked by frequent arguments.

One day the husband visited a friend in a hospital's intensive care unit. There he saw patients who were so sick and weak that they couldn't breathe without the help of respirators. It suddenly struck the husband how fortunate he was to have a healthy wife.

That night when the wife came home and began to unload on him, the husband just kept smiling at her as if he was appreciating and discovering something wonderful. She was puzzled (this behavior was beyond the comprehension of her habitual domain), but on this evening the usual argument did not develop.

"What's going on?" she finally asked her husband. He described the plight of the patients in intensive care, his gratefulness that his wife had avoided such a fate, and how much he loved her.

The wife was moved by this and admitted that she loved her husband as well. The pair became best friends and the marriage thrived.

It happened because the husband was willing to change his habitual domain from the usual angry reciprocation to gratitude. This, in turn, led to a profound change in his wife's behavior.

its passing, as a rabbit leaves its tracks in snow. The Hebrew people described God's voice as the sound of the whirlwind. Native Americans saw the Sky Spirit in the shadow of a flying eagle sweeping across the prairie grass.

A habitual domain is no different, really. It cannot be directly observed, but it can be described, examined, pictured, visualized, understood. It can be seen indirectly in three dimensions:

- Behavior functions, such as goal setting, state evaluation, charge structures, attention allocation. (Chapter 5)
- Concerned events, such as attention allocated to job, family, social interactions and health. (Chapter 6)
- External interactions, such as others within our identification spheres, our living domains, role maps and attitudes. (Chapter 6)

How Our Minds Operate

These three dimensions have vast implications which result from the operations of our minds. For the sake of remembering them, I have summarized them into four hypotheses of the mind.

GOAL SETTING AND STATE EVALUATION

Each one of us has a set of goal functions, and for each goal function we have an ideal state, or an equilibrium point, we want to reach and maintain (this is goal setting). We continuously monitor, consciously or subconsciously, where we are relative to that ideal state (this is state evaluation).

Goal setting and state evaluation are dynamic, interactive and subject to all kinds of forces. These include:

- *physiological condition* — our health can affect our goal setting.
- *self-suggestion* — confidence and power depend on what we say to ourselves.
- *external information* — much of what we do depends

Many people believe that everything happens for a reason, or that from every event we can derive some meaning. This self-analysis occurs most often in dramatic situations. Are there times when you have felt this way? Was it a good feeling?

on information that comes to us from outside ourselves.
- *memory* — everything we have learned is part of our behavior and decision making.
- *our capacity to process information* — people have different methods and abilities to use what they learn to solve problems.

CHARGE STRUCTURE AND ATTENTION ALLOCATION

Each event in our lives is related to a set of goal functions in our brains. When the event deviates from what we perceive as ideal, the goal functions will produce various levels of charge. All together these charges make up our charge structure, and this can change dynamically. At any given point in time, our attention will be paid to the event that has the most influence on our charge structure, either because it is the most urgent or the most deeply ingrained.

RELEASING CHARGE

To release charges, we tend to select the action that leads to the lowest remaining charge. We will never release all charges, even when we are sleeping, because the brain continues actively processing information and ideas. A person is most comfortable and happiest when charges are reduced to a comparatively low level. This can be partly accomplished by using our minds to see the charges that affect us as being positive forces.

INFORMATION INPUT

Humans have innate needs to know or to gather external information. Mental focus helps us gather the information we need. Even when some information comes at us randomly, by paying attention we can process it productively. If we do not pay attention to it, the arriving external information will not be processed in our mind.

How Our Brains
Process Information

Exactly how our brains process information, handle charges, evaluate circumstances and set goals is still a mystery. But neurophysiology and psychology have provided lots of clues. Four hypotheses sum up the neuro-information processes that affect our habitual domains. I call these hypotheses, because no one completely understands the miracles of the human brain yet.

CIRCUIT PATTERN HYPOTHESIS

Thoughts, concepts or ideas are represented by circuit patterns in the brain that are reinforced when the ideas are repeatedly used or rehearsed. The stronger the circuit patterns (the more often used), the more easily the corresponding thoughts are retrieved in our thinking and decision making process.

A good example: You drive the same route home from work so often that if you don't make a conscious decision to change your route, you will find your way home on "auto pilot" while you are really thinking about other things than the direction you are driving.

To apply this hypothesis to your life, think periodically about the experience of your successes. Let these happy events occupy your brain to make you feel good and confident (because success breeds confidence).

UNLIMITED CAPACITY HYPOTHESIS

Each normal brain has a practically unlimited capacity for encoding and storing all the thoughts and concepts that its owner will ever need. All evidence points to the fact that the capacity of our brains far exceeds even our ability to imagine that capacity.

To prove your brain's capacity to encode new and different ideas quickly and effectively, try this exercise. Think of a person you are afraid of or are nervous about meeting. In your mind's eye, see that person reduced to one-tenth of his or her size. Do it again. Now the person is less than 1 inch tall. Visualize the tiny person jumping into your palm. You could let him change forms or dance etc. Repeat this several times. Then open your eyes. You will find that your fear or nervousness about the meeting has disappeared because the person is no larger than your palm and is subject to your control. Why can you do this? Because you have unlimited capacity to change your mind and what you think.

EFFICIENT RESTRUCTURING HYPOTHESIS

Encoded ideas are organized systematically, like data bases, for efficient retrieval and are continuously restructured according to the dictation of our attention. In this way relevant ideas can be efficiently retrieved to release charges.

While computers take time to reprogram, our brains do it instantaneously and constantly. Some of this restructuring goes without our notice; other times we cause it to happen. Here's a quick exercise to show you how this works:

When you are very angry about something, restructure your thinking like this. Take 10 or more deep breaths. Hold the inhaled breath for as long as you can; exhale and keep your lungs empty as long as you can. As you repeat the process you will find you cannot hold in mind whatever it was that was annoying you. The deep breathing is signaling to your brain, "I need oxygen!" Obtaining the oxygen becomes uppermost in your brain's attention as it tries to meet the body's need. At the end of 10 breaths, your mind will most likely be empty of the annoyance. To get it back, you will have to purposely recall it, again restructuring your brain's activity.

ANALOGY/ASSOCIATION HYPOTHESIS

When confronted with a new event, the brain first investigates its features and attributes to establish a relationship to things the brain already knows. Once the relationship is established, the whole of past knowledge is brought to bear on understanding the new event.

The *positive* aspect of this brain scan is the value of accumulated experience. If our brains did not work this way, we would never amass enough knowledge to be competent. The *negative* aspect is that we can bring baggage or old ideas to new experiences. If we aren't careful, we can

Challenge your creativity and the flexibility of your habitual domain. Think up five new products you believe people might buy.

reject experiences and knowledge that would benefit us because we are resting on old information.

Almost all human behavior can be explained by these two sets of hypotheses (how our mind operates and how our brain processes information), including the behavior tendencies described in Chapter 3.

Properties Of Habitual Domains

Once we have grasped how the brain works to create a habitual domain, and how it is structured, we can see its properties. Understanding these properties can help us understand some of the most mystifying aspects of our own thoughts and behavior. Then we can move toward positive change and releasing our potential.

Within a person's habitual domain are usually four pairs of contrasting and paradoxical properties.

SIMPLICITY / COMPLEXITY

If you are old enough to read this, you already have an untold number of strong and useful circuit patterns in your brain. You are capable of making a great many judgments. For example, if you see someone crying, you may reasonably assume that they are sad. If they are laughing, it means they are happy, or at least amused. These patterns are so much a part of you that they seem simple. But every simple pattern is really the surface of complex understanding or knowledge.

Superficially, the whole concept of habitual domain may seem all too simple and obvious. But if you oversimplify it, you will lose your curiosity and will to explore, and thus will never really discover what wonders it contains.

Judging the message of habitual domain, or dismissing it as nothing new, will close your mind. And a closed mind will pay no attention, let alone make new discoveries.

For proof of this you need look no further than the typical American marriage. Statistically, couples in the U.S. are most likely to divorce in the first two years of marriage or when the partners are in middle age.

"Simplifying" makes it easier for us to cope with daily problems; "complexifying" makes us appreciate the uniqueness and marvel of each HD. Therefore, let us properly embrace the simplicity and treasure the complexity of HD.

Why? Consider that a newly wedded couple usually find each other new, exciting and attractive. But after a period of time, being together becomes monotonous. After one or two years the desire to know one another and the interest in each other is lowered because of oversimplification and the feeling that nothing new is happening.

Couples hoping to overcome this difficulty must open their minds to discovering new things about one another. Since there are no two identical individuals or habitual domains, there is plenty to learn even about someone with whom we are intimate. And by learning more about another person, we are expanding our own habitual domain.

In fact, there is no way you could ever completely understand your spouse's habitual domain. That means there will always be a sense of mystery about that person, and something new to discover.

STABILITY/DYNAMICS

On one hand, a **stable** habitual domain represents maturity and experience. On the other, it can mean rigid, fixed and unchanging thought patterns which stifle mental growth.

Stability represents maturity and efficiency for solving routine problems; dynamics is needed for coping with challenging problems and remaining flexible. Therefore, let us properly embrace the stability and treasure the dynamics of HD.

The word **dynamic** means "changing with time." Habitual domain, especially the actual domain, is dynamic. At any one time, a variety of ideas and operators might be combining in our actual domain. But unless we encounter extraordinary circumstances and previously unexperienced events, it's difficult to change or expand our potential domain, which is the total of all our existing ideas and operators. To do that we must encounter something new.

Not all of us can travel to exotic places or have intimate encounters with great minds. But reading good books, tackling new projects, even talking with new people are examples of effective ways of expanding your potential domain.

Nature reminds us that close examination reveals marvelous complexity in every living thing.

Suspending our dependence on our actual domain and allowing possibilities in is important to every individual. But companies can also benefit from the willingness to change.

By the mid-1960s, Universal Studios was the biggest movie corporation in the United States. About that time, one of the company's vice presidents suggested that the firm invest in Florida, where the costs of both real estate and wages were

154

lower. But this represented a major break with tradition. Other company officials noted that Universal was tops in the industry and was in excellent financial condition. Their attitude was, "Why should we change when everything is fine?"

The proposal was shelved.

Shortly afterward, the Walt Disney Company discovered the advantages of Florida and made a huge investment there. Walt Disney World is now the world's number one tourist attraction.

Today Disney is a much bigger company than Universal. Because of Universal's misplaced belief in its position and stability, it was surpassed by its competitor.

CONSISTENCY/ CONTRARINESS

Consistency is very reassuring. It makes us feel comfortable and peaceful. But it is **Contrariness** that pushes us to expand our habitual domains.

For example, contradiction emerges when a company tries to cut production costs while improving product quality. Conventional wisdom holds that better quality requires more time and higher capital investment, which would seem to be contrary to lowering costs.

Consistency makes us feel good; contrariness offers us the opportunity to expand our HD. Therefore, let us properly embrace the consistency and treasure the contrariness of HD.

This contradiction presents a challenge and, perhaps, will drive us to discover new processes to resolve it. Henry Ford revolutionized the automobile business by introducing techniques of mass production and standardization that made autos affordable to most individuals while generating substantial profits.

A good leader must understand the need for contrariness and seize the opportunity when it occurs. An individual needs the courage to do the same. Facing the contradictions that experience offers us takes determination and courage, but each contradiction represents a chance for breaking through constraining limits.

Beauty can be seen only because there is ugliness.
Good can be known because there is evil.
— Lao Tzu

ABSORPTION/REJECTION OF EXTERNAL INFORMATION

It's considerably more trouble to absorb new information and ideas than to reject them. Acceptance means our brain has to encode and restructure our existing memory so that the

new information can be integrated into our past experiences.

This is a time-consuming and laborious task. Only those individuals willing to open their minds and expand their habitual domains will initiate this complicated effort.

Also remember that it is best not to rush to judgment. Making a judgment usually means coming to a conclusion; thereafter we are likely to close our minds to any new observations or information.

"Other people may be right" is a valuable concept. If you accept it, your mind will always be open and willing to question. You won't be reluctant to ask the questions that offer you the potential to learn from others.

Examining the anatomy of your habitual domain is, like studying human physical anatomy, enormously fascinating. But it is not the study itself that is the goal, rather the use that can be made of it. Understanding our physical anatomy gives us ways to be healthier and more physically capable. Understanding the anatomy of our habitual domain gives us ways to be more capable in everything we do and become.

Understanding is ideal. But even without full understanding, we can control our behavior and thought processes to allow growth and positive change.

Learning the anatomy of your habitual domain is just a tool, like so much of the rest of this book. Its value is to get you where you deserve to go — toward the full realization of yourself. That realization can be found as you strive toward the Ideal Habitual Domain. This ideal calls to all of us, and in our individual ways all of us can reach it in some measure.

Absorption of external information takes time and effort and can expand our HD, while rejection of that insulates us from the increasing interference of the external world. Therefore, let us properly embrace the absorption and treasure the rejection.

Children absorb external information quickly. As we grow older, the process is more laborious.

邁向理想的習慣領域

Chapter 10

Reaching Toward the Ideal Habitual Domain

Why make the commitment to understand and expand your own habitual domain?

Will it make you rich? Happy? Wise? Successful? Yes, it can.

If you're determined to earn your first million by a certain age or to become president of your company, working on your habitual domain will help get you there — or as close as you personally can be. Understanding the power of habitual domains can help you achieve any goal you set.

But more importantly, being aware of your habitual domain will provide something enormously valuable — and more difficult to gain than wealth for many people: *a sense of balance in your life.*

We've all heard stories of business and professional people, entertainers and others who fought furiously to reach a particular goal, but found once they had achieved it that they were somehow dissatisfied. For all their accomplishments, they felt oddly incomplete.

A person who truly understands his or her habitual domain will certainly be capable of achieving fame, fortune and power. If those are the goals you set for yourself, knowing your habitual domain will be part of your success in reaching them.

But you will also maintain a balance, a sense of stability

Create the ideal job and the ideal state of the company in which you would like to work. How is it different from your present job? How will you implement changes to bring your present work life closer to your ideal?

(financial, emotional, spiritual) that will see you through almost anything.

This is not to say that if you diligently develop your habitual domain, no harm ever will befall you. Reversals and losses — both in business and in life — are everyone's fate.

But for the earnest habitual domain practitioner, reversals and other temporary setbacks will be offset by the deeply satisfying pleasures and accomplishments that accompany a healthy, flexible, growing habitual domain.

An Unchanging Domain

In any situation a number of outcomes could possibly occur, but only one outcome actually does occur.

Similarly, our habitual domain can be classified into our **Potential Domain** (possible outcomes) and **Actual Domain** (actual outcome). The former is the collection of all ideas and operators that can potentially occur; the latter is those ideas and operators that actually become activated in our minds.

If you have no knowledge of, say, microbiology, you have no circuit patterns representing ideas about microbiology. Thus, microbiology is not part of your potential domain.

But as soon as you read a book or article dealing with microbiology, or see a TV documentary on the subject, then you absorb that information into your potential domain. Even if you cannot consciously remember it, it remains there in your brain (at least it does until the corresponding circuit patterns are wiped out because too many neurons have died).

When you *can* consciously draw upon that information it becomes part of your actual domain at that moment.

Of course, the potential and actual domains are always in flux, with ideas and operators shifting back and forth from one to the other. Neither is permanent and unchanging.

The only unchanging domain would be an ideal habitual domain. The ideal habitual domain represents an enormous sphere of awareness and understanding. To possess it means one has achieved a nearly godlike state.

Those who possess an ideal habitual domain have *potential* domains that can identify with all people and all living things, that can understand all events and problems. Their *actual* domains are extremely liquid and flexible, with the power to solve any problems instantaneously.

Such an ideal habitual domain would release our individual frustrations and those of others. It represents thinking and behavior of an extraordinarily vital, powerful and creative nature. A person with this habitual domain would be welcome everywhere — free from hatred, anger, jealousy, sorrow, frustration and depression.

No doubt, very few human beings have accomplished this. Many sages in the East and West may have had HDs close to this ideal. Persons with a particular religious commitment might say that Jesus or Buddha or Mohammed were human examples of ideal HDs, and the God you worship, no matter what your religion, must have an ideal HD. Perhaps no one else has come close.

Nonetheless, it is the goal toward which we should be striving. Simply the effort of striving to reach an ideal habitual domain can enormously enrich and expand our potential and actual habitual domains. Almost all religious thought is based on this principle of reaching toward a perfection perhaps mortally unattainable

After years of thought on the subject, I've come up with a list of features that would be enjoyed by the ideal habitual domain:

The **Potential Domain** of the ideal habitual domain must be broad enough to contain all the concepts allowing us to comprehend everything in the universe and the universe itself.

An ideal habitual domain's **Actual Domain** must be fluid, flexible, spontaneous, peaceful and potent. It's always ready to respond instantly, spontaneously and powerfully to help us solve our problems.

I realize that this goal is well out of our reach. If we spent every moment of every day poring over books in a library we couldn't hope to absorb that much information in a lifetime.

The idea is to do what we can with the time we've got.

The ideal habitual domain must be deep, with concentration and focus. It allows us to understand the details and depth of every concept. It also must be integrated so that concepts are systematically organized.

It must have a high degree of self-containment, already

The ideal habitual domain is like a great library which contains every volume ever printed and every idea ever thought. What's more, the ideal HD instantaneously can retrieve the right pieces of information we require precisely when we need them.

Seven Operators

EMPOWERMENT (GOAL SETTING)

1. **Self-image:**
   You are a unique creation and the transformation of
   the divine; so am I. Respect us both.
2. **Self-empowering:**
   Clear and specific goals produce the energy for your life; be
   committed to learning and doing with confidence.

MEANING (STATE EVALUATIONS)

3. **Events:**
   In everything that comes to your life, there are reasons. One of the
   main reasons is to help you grow and develop. Enjoy and learn
   from experience.
4. **Work:**
   Every task is part of your mission; your work can bring happiness.
   Bring enthusiasm and trust to your mission.

ATTITUDE

5. **Living domains:**
   You are the owner of your living domain; take responsibility for
   whatever occurs in it.
6. **Gratitude:**
   Appreciate life; be grateful for every experience; contribute to
   society.

LIFE AND TIME

7. **Your life:**
   Your life is the here and now. Enjoy it 100 percent and make
   a 100 percent contribution.

holding all the concepts and knowledge needed, so that it can detach itself from external influences as seen fit.

Finally it must be simple.

Now I imagine you are really incredulous. How can all this be **simple**?

But an ideal habitual domain would be simple. Like light and air, the ideal habitual domain exists simply, peacefully and inconspicuously.

An ideal habitual domain is **absorbing**. It accepts and digests all arriving ideas and concepts, and it absorbs and releases all incoming charges and frustrations.

It's **non-judgmental**. It holds no prejudice and does not allow itself to judge right or wrong on arriving events. (It may predict the outcome of such events, but that's a different matter than judging them.)

An ideal habitual domain is **free** and detached from the desires and wishes of the self. By forgetting the self, it thinks without predetermined conclusions and the restriction of assumptions.

It's **rich**. It can identify with and appreciate anything that exists in the world and the universe.

And finally, the ideal habitual domain **loves**. No ideal habitual domain can be without love. The perfect habitual domain has room within it to love all human beings and, for that matter, all the living things in the universe.

The Elusive Goal

Although each of us has unlimited capacity, many events continuously limit us, preventing us from reaching an ideal habitual domain. The need humans feel to reach an ideal is reflected in the windows of all the centuries of human thought, handed down in proverbs, texts, schools, common sense and great systems of belief such as Christianity, Islam, Buddhism, Judaism and Taoism. In developing the concepts of Habitual Domains, I have identified seven self-perpetuating operators that help us strive toward an ideal habitual domain.

Seven Self-Perpetuating Operators

We've already seen the tools represented by eight expansion methods (Chapter 7), nine principles for deep knowledge (Chapter 4), and letting our brain and behavior work for us (Chapter 8). Now we turn to the **seven self-perpetuating operators,** methods, principles and ideas that can change our minds in positive ways.

In the discussion that follows, keep in mind that you should not judge whether the operators as described are right or wrong. Indeed, you may find yourself philosophically disagreeing with the operators as stated.

Don't let that dissuade you from taking them seriously.

Just as the plus and minus operators in mathematics help us to arrive at another set of numbers, the following operators, the circuit patterns, are not right or wrong, but they can help us to reach another set of ideas or concepts.

These operators are self-perpetuating because once they are implanted in your habitual domain and used they will continuously grow and help you expand and enrich your habitual domain toward the ideal. Of all the ideas I have shared in this book , these are the most important.

1. Everyone is a priceless living entity. *We all are unique creations who carry the spark of the divine.*

If you're an atheist or an agnostic you're probably readying a protest. Even if you regard yourself as a religious person, you may be uncomfortable with that statement.

First, try to overcome the circuit patterns that may be set off by the use of words like "divine." Don't pass judgment on these operators. Let them go into your mind and feel the possibilities.

Consider that in Alcoholics Anonymous recovering substance abusers are asked to call upon a "higher power" in their battle against addiction. This does not mean that every AA member is religious.

But within the structure of AA, members find that whether they believe in God or not, they must at some point admit that on their own they have been powerless to control their addictive behavior. Thus they are asked to rely on a "higher power" — whether you call it God, the superego, dedication to family or whatever — to provide strength and hope.

That's the same attitude to assume in this discussion of operators.

Let's talk for a moment about the idea that everyone is a priceless living entity. We don't have to talk in religious terms. We can discuss it in business terms.

Suppose you were offered $1 million for your eyes. Would you take it?

What if someone wanted to buy your limbs? Or your heart or kidneys? What would they be worth to you?

Of course you'd never sell vital parts of your own body. They are priceless to you.

You are priceless. So is everybody else.

Once this idea of the pricelessness of yourself and every other living person becomes such a strong circuit pattern as to be a core element of your belief system, it will be the source of tremendous power.

The motivational speaker Zig Ziglar asks: If you have a race horse worth $1 million, would you let it drink alcohol, smoke, stay awake all night or be poisoned by drugs?

Isn't your priceless body worth the care you'd lavish on a race horse?

It's not just our bodies that require nurturing. Our minds (and souls, if you will) require it as well. In fact, we must be wary of establishing destructive circuit patterns.

If reading the biography of a great person can result in our incorporating some of that person's habitual domain into our own, then one must assume that hours devoted to violent entertainments, destructive gossip or pornography will result in those negative forces forming circuit patterns as well.

Ziglar notes that if someone dumped garbage in our living rooms we'd be furious, but that daily we unwittingly pollute our minds with intellectual garbage. Do you monitor the food for thought you incorporate into your habitual domain?

Do you allow time in each day to clean the garbage out of your mind with prayer or meditation or contemplation of nature and beauty so that your mind can grow in tranquillity?

Once this operator has been established in your habitual

Develop a plan to expand your HD in one of your most prejudiced areas. Ask someone else for an opinion you have prejudged as invalid and note his or her response to your asking. Use the solicited opinion in your plan and document a positive change. Note how this changes your relationship with that person.

domain, you'll find your attitude toward others will go through a profound change.

If we're all sparks of the divine (I often say that we are all "transformed from God or Buddha"), then on a very basic level we all are equals. Because of that awareness, I try to be polite and humble to others, to listen to their ideas and problems.

Personally, I believe that God or Buddha may sometimes be testing me through others. When a person aggravates or challenges me, I try to respond as if I were being tested in some ultimate way.

But even if you do not share my attitude, there are very pragmatic reasons for treating others well. If you're good to them, they will reciprocate and be good to you. This can lead to lives of joy and fortune for all.

In my own experience I've found this operator reaps huge benefits. For example, I've won teaching awards, which might seem unlikely given that my classes are in quantitative methods (not exactly a favorite of students) and I speak with a pronounced accent as a result of a childhood spent in Taiwan.

But I try to treat my students well, and they respond — both by giving me their support and friendship and by learning.

It's not always easy. After every exam I'll have a few students who storm into my office because they received poor grades. The exam was unfair, they'll usually say.

In most instances it's all too apparent why these students got poor marks — they didn't do the work. And I'm tempted to respond in a brusque and impatient manner.

But I quickly remind myself that these unhappy students also are "transformations of God or Buddha," and that I must be polite.

Once this operator is activated (meaning that it enters my actual domain), I become patient and feel that even this combative encounter holds the possibility for encouraging the student both to look honestly at his or her performance and to pump up enthusiasm for learning in the future.

This operator works not only for personal development but also for the development of organizational culture. It can make you well liked by your colleagues. If everyone in your organization could subscribe to this operator, how wonderful would be your work environment. Eventually this would lead to higher productivity, profitability and satisfaction.

2. Clear, specific and challenging goals produce energy for our lives. *I am totally committed to doing and learning with confidence.* This is the only way I can reach the goals.

Without goals, we are adrift. We have no control over our destinies. Instead we are blown about by the wind, or carried wherever the current runs.

Imagine, though, that you are rowing a boat across an ocean strait. If you have a clear destination and you know how far you are from it, then the charge of reaching your goal can be transformed into drive. You will continuously row until you reach your goal. You won't lose your confidence, give up or drift. But if you have no idea where the shore may be, keeping on may become impossible.

Goals energize us. They fill us with vitality. But to be effective they must be:

- Clear
- Specific
- Measurable
- Reachable
- Challenging

This last point is important, since it's human nature to take it easy on ourselves. If your goals are too low, the generated charge and drive won't be significant. Even when you reach such a goal, you may not feel much satisfaction.

Specific goals are vital because in the rush of daily events we may find ourselves being attracted to randomly arriving goals and desires. We may even be controlled by them if we lack a clear focus on just what it is we hope to accomplish.

But with a clear, specific and challenging goal, we create a high level of charge that focuses our efforts. We won't be distracted by randomly arriving events.

Developing Confidence

Let's talk about **confidence**. Without it, you may abandon your goals. You'll be fearful and miserable. With it, you can

Think of your top three current goals. Do you have a reward system for each goal? Does it motivate you? If not, choose another reward. Establish a time frame and a measurable amount of improvement for each goal.

光明心態

佛帝化身萬事助長

全責主人全力知行

使命樂園感恩布施

標標清明秒秒生光

游伯龍

accomplish things you never thought possible. Here are five ways to increase your confidence:

- Keep learning. As you increase your abilities and knowledge, your confidence will grow as well.
- Develop a good working attitude. Instead of throwing in the towel at the first sign of difficulty, develop your perseverance and persistence.
- Develop as many good relationships with as many good people as you can. It's simple networking — you'll be creating more sources and channels for useful information, not to mention building a support system of friends and colleagues who can help you get through tough times.
- Break down your goals into small, measurable and achievable subgoals. Finish each of these subgoals one by one. At each step in the process you will increase your confidence and abilities. You may even want to celebrate these milestone victories to enhance your confidence.
- Do it. Don't wait until you know all the facts. You'll never know all the facts.

The fact is that most challenging problems, by definition, lie outside our existing domain of knowledge. That's why they pose a challenge.

Since we're dealing at least in part with unknowns, we cannot know ahead of time everything we might encounter on the journey to our goal. But if we're adequately armed with knowledge, confidence and a general blueprint of action, then we can begin to execute it.

Yes, this involves risk. But without taking risks we cannot explore our potential. Taking risks is an essential part of exploring and expanding our domains. After all, we learn even from our failures. Through the confidence we have gained by learning and doing, the charge generated by taking risk can be transformed into drive.

3. There are reasons for everything that occurs. *One major reason is to help us grow and develop.*

Because I carry the divine spark (since I am transformed

Consider five decisions you made recently. Describe their outcomes. How did imagined outcomes affect the actions you took?

Bright and Positive Mentality
- *I am a unique creation of God or Buddha; everything occurs to help me grow.*
- *I am the owner of my life; I take full responsibility and commit myself totally to learning and action.*
- *My work is my life mission and enjoyment. Wherever I go, I appreciate and pay back society.*
- *Each goal is specific and clear; every second of my life produces enlightenment.*
(*translation of poem, page 168*)

from God or Buddha), everything that happens to me has a reason; *i.e.,* to help me grow and mature.

Therefore I must pay close attention to the events in my life. I must be concerned and look for understanding.

When firmly established, this circuit pattern encourages us to take advantage of the events in our lives, to use them to expand our habitual domains.

Now I fully realize that many readers may believe that the world operates in a random fashion, that in fact things happen for no apparent reason. Look at events from your individual perspective. What is the sense that can be made in your life of an experience or occurrence? The "reason" something occurs may not be a sweeping cosmic rationale, but something that will differ from person to person.

Remember, you don't have to fully agree with each of these operators, only give them a chance.

Let's talk for a moment about **failure**. Nobody likes it, but everybody experiences it.

As commonly defined, failure is a situation in which less than satisfying events have occurred to affect our performance and produce an outcome less than expected. This narrow definition is dangerous. The very thought of failure can bring on depression and erode our confidence.

But it needn't be the case. We can avoid these feelings if we're able to turn failure into a success — even a limited success.

Scientists working on research say they may learn nearly as much from an experiment that doesn't work as they do from one that does. If nothing else, they have eliminated one possible solution, freeing themselves to pursue others.

An unsatisfactory outcome should be regarded simply as a different type of meaningful experience. If you overreact to frustration and fear, your actual domain may be occupied by those negative emotions.

Don't let that happen. Every less-than-desirable event has some special meaning, some important lesson, some seed for success. In such a situation, don't give in to suffering; ask yourself what you can learn from the experience. Write it down. The very act of writing will make it positive and it will become a more permanent part of your habitual domain.

4. Every task is part of my life's mission. *I have the enthusiasm and confidence to accomplish this mission.*

Some people discover their mission in life and are able to find work that provides the necessary support for them and their families as well as for their mission. This is a wonderful state to be in, when work seems simply to be part of a person's reason for being, and achievements in work bring not only monetary gain but great spiritual or emotional rewards.

Not everyone is so fortunate. Sometimes understanding our life's mission takes many years. Sometimes we see the goal and must work toward it through setbacks and challenges. Sometimes the work is very hard and even if we see it as part of a mission, the hardship itself is daunting.

Nonetheless, all the work we do is important. In fact, *everything* we do matters. Basically, there is no such thing as an unimportant task. We must regard every task as important to our lives. Whatever we are doing at a given moment is occupying 100 percent of our lives at that time. We must learn to say, *All my life is being given right now to what I am doing. I must do this as though it were worth taking up my life.*

Once this operator has taken root in your habitual domain, you will find that it flowers in very positive ways:

- You'll approach each job with a total dedication of mind and effort.
- You'll experience feelings of accomplishment and satisfaction. This, of course, further builds up your confidence.
- Your abilities will become apparent to others. This is gratifying, but more is at stake than having your ego stroked. Others will respect you for your efforts and will rely on you. This, in turn, will increase your opportunities to help others solve their problems. By doing that, you will be offered more opportunity, simultaneously serving your own goals as you build up more skills, knowledge and confidence.

Whatever tasks engage most of your attention — employment, creating art or music, studies, building a company, sustaining a home and raising children, or some combination of these — comprise a major part of your habitual domain. All

Most people will choose goals within their habitual domains. Imagine a situation where you are forced to choose a goal outside your HD. How could it help you?

these tasks can be made more manageable and more meaningful by applying the concepts you have learned in this book.

But the most important thing to remember is that your "work" is your life. Living a good life — a life that fulfills your potential and shares it with society — is your primary occupation, and it deserves your very best. If the tasks that engage you right now are not the ones you really want to do over time, then set about to change them. Even while you are working toward change, however, it is important to apply your very best efforts to what is at hand.

Remember, what you are doing in any given moment is *your life*. You deserve that it be done superbly.

Most people want to find enjoyable work, but they forget that the joy is here and now by changing the meaning of the work or actual domain. Say "I want to enjoy it" for the task you dislike. Your brain will restructure to make it enjoyable, or at least less dislikable (please review chapter 8).

5. I am the owner of my living domain. I *take responsibility for everything that happens in it.*

We are the masters of the domains wherein we live, act and connect with the outside world. Therefore, we must take responsibility — that is, agree to be a positive force — in every thing within our world. We cannot simply let things happen around us and expect to succeed at reaching our own potential.

At a fundamental level, we all know this. The Nike company has had such success with its slogan "Just Do It" because at some level we all know we must act if we are to change for the better.

The work we do has value when we bring to it our best efforts.

When this circuit pattern or belief becomes strong, it will push you on to a keener understanding of your habitual domain. You'll be willing to take the initiative to be your best self.

Taking responsibility is a sign of maturity. Individuals unwilling to take charge of events and be responsible for their actions generally have closed minds. Their habitual domains lack flexibility and are difficult to expand.

In my teaching career I've identified basically two types of student. The first actively participates and is willing to take charge. The second tries to steer clear of social or extracurric-

Who Owns This Land?

Some years back my wife and I purchased a small farm outside Lawrence, Kansas, near Clinton Reservoir. It's been our regular weekend retreat ever since.

One summer night after the sun had gone down and it was nearly time for bed, I wandered out of the house and about the farm, absolutely delighted with the cool breeze rustling the tree branches, the stars in the cloudless night sky and the reflection of moonlight on the nearby lake.

And, to tell the truth, I was feeling rather proud that this property belonged to me.

That started me thinking about the very concept of ownership. Legally, of course, I own my farm. Yet I also realize that in 5 or 10 or 20 years it will pass on to someone else. I certainly cannot take it with me wherever I may go.

On that beautiful summer night I realized that at best I was a temporary trustee of the land.

These musings led to further thoughts. For example, who owned the lake? Technically, it was public property, but was I enjoying the view any less because I did not hold personal ownership of the water and shoreline? No. I appreciated the view, and that was enough.

Who owned the moon? A ridiculous question, perhaps, but here again, anyone who appreciated the moon was in a sense its owner.

The close connection between appreciation and ownership has grown stronger with me over the years. For example, I believe your spouse isn't truly your spouse unless you actively appreciate him or her. Your business customers can't truly be called your customers unless you value and appreciate them.

Similarly, individuals who have truly developed their powers of appreciation are rich whatever the condition of their bank accounts.

ular activities and avoids responsibility whenever possible.

The first student learns through his or her experiences and will establish beneficial relations with others; the second often is isolated and has little opportunity to learn about and understand his fellow humans. These two types of approach are not limited to university students.

The implications of this in a business setting are obvious. A manager who is unwilling to take charge and be responsible for his subordinates will find that those subordinates will not commit themselves completely to their work. This initiates a vicious circle.

If an employee tries to avoid responsibility, a boss will be reluctant to assign challenging tasks. Denied the chance to excel and to perform, such an employee will find advancement opportunities extremely limited.

Using the tools you've learned, evaluate the HDs of five clients, competitors, contacts and colleagues. Evaluate the HDs of five family members, friends and fellow committee or club members.

6. Be appreciative and grateful, and don't forget to give back to society.
This world is full of beautiful living things, scenery and events. At a simple level, *we must never fail to appreciate the world around us* that reminds us every day how precious life is.

Appreciation, gratification and making contributions are all circuit patterns, modes of behavior which can be cultivated until they become second nature.

They benefit us first, because such circuit patterns make us feel good. But they also benefit others. Through reciprocation, by making a contribution and giving back some of what we have gained we will assure that our circuit patterns create an upward spiral of joy and satisfaction that affects not only ourselves but those around us.

Do you think that sounds too good to be true? It works. The sharp rise of volunteering in America is due to the fact that people receive immeasurable satisfaction from helping others.

On a simple level, when you receive compliments, make sure you reciprocate to show your appreciation. It is important to say "Thank you."

When others complain about something you've done, your first response may be resentment. Don't fall into that trap. As hard as it may be, try to appreciate an opportunity to improve yourself. View their criticism as a form of encouragement. Thank them for sharing their views.

The Elusive Goal

Let's admit from the start that it is unlikely that you or I will ever achieve an ideal HD. Such a state of wisdom, contentment and achievement is likely to be reached only by a very few. To be in this state for an extended time would be to achieve the true "enlightenment" spoken of in many revered, or holy, texts the world around. It is a state that belongs to sages or to saints.

Nevertheless, virtually all of us have at some point in our lives — even if only for a minute or two —experienced a flash of our own ideal HD.

It could have occurred in a moment of immense satisfaction when difficulties are overcome, when our best self has been offered and accepted, when we have realized our tremendous capacity for forgiveness and wisdom, for love, concern and sharing.

In such moments we know a supremely gratifying sense of harmony and well-being.

A person with a large HD will know these moments more often than his or her fellows because he or she has more resources, knowledge and ideas to draw on. Such a person sees the potential for solving problems and creating harmony in many situations and relationships. Wisdom, success and inner peace are built on this harmony.

Moving beyond personal relationships, I believe it is imperative that those of us who have benefited from society give something back.

Those of us with money can give money. Those of us with skills and knowledge can contribute those. The important thing is to share what we have gained.

7. Our remaining lifetime is our most valuable asset. I *want to enjoy it 100 percent and make a 100 percent contribution to society in each moment of my remaining life.*

Time is ticking continuously. When the time comes, we all return to the Great Nature, no matter how valuable your body and life are now. Without life, our body becomes useless. Therefore, our remaining lifetime is our most valuable asset. There are two notorious ways of wasting time. One is to regret, resent or feel guilty over something we've done or have failed to do.

"If I'd done things differently, I wouldn't be suffering today."

Such regrets only waste precious time, depress us and rob us of confidence, leaving us unable to enjoy our lives fully.

Another time-waster is worrying about the future and the accompanying hesitation. Worry is often the result of a fear of taking risks. We're afraid of making the wrong decision.

Trouble is, challenges usually aren't all that clear at the very beginning. Uncertainty and the unknown have a tendency to unfold gradually. We learn by doing. If you wait until you have all the facts, it may be too late to do anything.

Some of us go through life unwilling to risk anything. We end up doing little. We might feel safe in our very limited domain, but we're not going to accomplish very much. Put aside worry. You likely will extend your life. In any case, the life that remains will be more meaningful.

When you say to yourself that you want to enjoy your lifetime here and now and make a 100 percent contribution to society in each moment of your remaining life, your brain will restructure your circuit patterns, allowing you more likelihood to do so. Your life and habitual domain will consequently be expanded and enriched. Enjoy your life and make your contributions here and now.

You can't see your HD. You can't touch it or hear it or smell it.

But it's always there, omnipresent, affecting your behavior in thousands of big and little ways.

You can ignore it and live as a slave to the circuit patterns that you don't even recognize.

Or you can seize control and become the master. This is the choice faced by every thinking man and woman.

Compare a day of your regular activities currently and a day a year ago. How has your habitual domain changed? Did you mainly expand your HD or did you reinforce patterns you already had?

Appendix 1

EFFECTIVE GOAL SETTING FOR CAREER MANAGEMENT

- **Find a quiet place where no one will call or disturb you.**

Make yourself as comfortable and relaxed as possible. If you like, put on some soothing music. Try to relax your entire body.

- **Get in touch with your own world and explore your potential domain.**

Be a serious archaeologist of yourself. Explore and understand your habitual domain. Review Chapters 5 and 6, if necessary. The following suggestions can help you keep a positive focus.

1. Remember your past, especially when you were young. Did you think then about accomplishing something great in your lifetime, such as being a great inventor, scientist, industrialist? What position and what kind of wealth did you envision for yourself? What sort of contribution did you see yourself making to the world?

2. Write down three or four of the most exciting and thrilling experiences in your past. Concentrate on successful events. At the moment of your greatest success and excitement, were you filled with confidence and a sense of achievement? Were your spirits high? Did others applaud and praise you? How did it feel, and did it help prepare you for your next challenge? Now write down some adverse events. What did you learn from them?

3. Search for the factors that most contributed to your success in those gratifying moments, such as: special knowledge, intelligence, perseverance, hard work, concentration, good human relationship skills, even luck. The more details the better.

4. Explore your physical and mental resources. Analyze your strengths and weaknesses. Catalogue the resources

Exploring your potential domain can lead you to heights you never imagined.

under your command on a piece of paper.

- **Let your actual domain work for you.**

Recall that to be effective, your goals must be clear, specific, measurable, reachable and challenging.

1. Suppose you could accomplish all the goals you set for yourself. What are those goals? Write them down separately on different pieces of paper. The more goals the better.

2. For each goal write down on the same piece of paper when you would like to accomplish it. Then write down the feeling, attitude and sensations you will experience when you achieve that goal. Compare that feeling with your current state. Does a charge develop?

3. On each goal write down the names of three or four persons who you think have accomplished those goals you stated. These can be historic individuals or people you are acquainted with. Study their biographies or observe their behavior, if needed.

4. Review your HD and the goals on which you wrote previously. Study and rank them carefully in terms of importance, urgency, feasibility and compatibility with your HD. Finally, decide which three or four goals you most want to achieve. Write down those goals clearly and concisely on a new piece of paper and challenge yourself to attain them.

- **Make a detailed plan.**

To build a good house we need a blueprint. To reach our goals we need a detailed plan.

1. Study how those people who have accomplished your goals did so. What kind of personality, attitude and methods did they use to overcome difficulty and frustrations? How did they develop and change their HDs and mentality in the process of attaining success? The answers will help you understand what it takes to reach your goals.

2. Learn the skills, knowledge, information and rela-

tionships you need to achieve your goals. What problems or obstacles now prevent you from reaching your goals?

3. Make a detailed plan by breaking down the big goals into a number of measurable, specific and reachable subgoals. Create a timetable showing when you will gain your needed set of skills, information and relationships. How would you overcome obstacles and difficulties over time? Execute your detailed plans step by step with total commitment and dedication.

4. Make daily, weekly, monthly and yearly measurable goals and plans to keep yourself accountable and to create charges for achievement. By planning and achievement you will be creating the life you desire.

- **Expand and enrich your habitual domain and execute the plan.**

Continuously review and rehearse your goals and plans; mentally experience the feelings, sensations, personality and habitual domain that you think you will have when you reach your goals.

This will build the strong circuit patterns which will in turn guide your behavior and thinking. It also will increase your confidence and maintain your focus.

Along the way, read good books. If you spent only 30 minutes a day in reading useful books, you would spend 170 hours studying in a year.

Every day try to discover three or more new concepts to help you achieve your goals.

Finally and most importantly, mobilize all your mental and physical resources to execute your plan. Without persistence, the plan can achieve nothing. While the plan may be refined and revised during execution, the goals should be steady and unchanging.

Don't give up. If you do, you are giving up your own goals and fulfillment, your own life.

Appendix 2

ORGANIZATIONAL HABITUAL DOMAINS

Every organization is, in effect, a living entity and therefore has its habitual domain. An organization is a dynamic decision mechanism, with information leading to goal setting and resulting charges. The charges determine attention allocation that leads to execution or implementation of some action.

To study organizational HD, we can look into these dimensions of an organization: shared values, cultures, attitudes, policies, day-to-day procedures and routines, financial structure, technical evolution, strategic planning, human resource management, leadership and interface with the external world.

Internally, the organization can also evaluate these seven dimensions: shared values, organizational structure, personnel staffing, growth strategy, management style, control systems and special skills or strengths.

Charted, the overall habitual domain of an organization might look something like this:

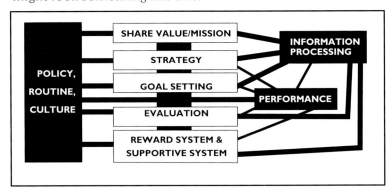

Organizational HDs can be studied in a way similar to our study of personal HDs. However, an organization is a collection of people who perform a set of tasks and work together to accomplish the goals of the organization. In turn, this allows the individuals to reach some of their own goals.

This interweaving of the group and the individual makes an organization's HD more complicated than a person's.

The three dimensions of personal HDs (Chapter 5-6) can be used to study the individual members' HD, and when these are appropriately aggregated, they can be used to study the organization's HD. In addition, the three dimensions and their sub-dimensions can also be used, with slight modifications if needed, to describe the organizational HDs.

Due to the special features of the organization, the following are worth special mention in our study of organizational HDs.

1. An organization is a collection of both sub-organizations and individual members.

Each sub-organization and individual member have their own unique HDs. For instance, in an ordinary corporation, the people in the marketing units may share some common traits (such as being extroverted, innovative, confident), which form an important part of the HD of the marketing unit. Similarly, the accounting unit has its unique HDs, including such attitudes as being precise, reserved and orderly.

In addition to the formal organization units, there are informal coalitions. In the extreme, the coalitions can be so strong that they become dominant in determining the organization's policies and decisions. Awareness of the existence of the organization units and informal coalitions, their unique HDs and their shared commonality will allow us to better understand the HD of the entire organization, including its charge structure, attention allocation, goal setting and state evaluation. Attention to the connectivity of information flows and decision processes among the members of the organization can help us identify the units or coalitions. In addition, incentives and reward systems also help us to see how an organization drives its employees to work.

2. Leadership and its moral influence on its members is important.

The organization has a set of tasks and jobs to be performed by its members to accomplish the goals and missions of the organization and its members. Like playing a sport or in a business, coordination, leadership and teamwork become extremely important for organizational success.

Good leadership should be able to identify the ideal states (HD) for the organization to move toward and be able to mobilize the members by creating charges, confidence and enthusiasm to reach the ideal. When moral influence is most effective, the members of the organization would wish to live and die with the leader for their common goals.

Planning, coordination (assigning right jobs to right people), careful execution, organization, government, reward and punishment are some basic tools that the leader can utilize to achieve the goals. Leadership, at its best, allows its members to fulfill their dreams and, at the same time, lets the organization reach its ideal. In this case the members may not even be aware of the existence of the leader.

A troop cannot fight and win without a good general. Likewise, an organization cannot be vital and successful without a good leader. To emphasize the importance of leadership, we may use leadership quality as a new dimension of the organizational HD. Leadership quality can be measured by (1) knowledge and wisdom, (2) courage and commitment, (3) sincerity and trustworthiness, (4) humanity and people skills and (5) discipline and control of the self and the organization.

A good leader, therefore, knows about his or her organization and the external environment. He or she knows what can and cannot be done. He or she has the courage to make hard choices and to make a commitment. People trust the leader who can mobilize people to reach the goals of the organization, which also translates into reaching goals of individuals. A good leader is good at self-discipline as well as good at governing his/her organization. The strong leader sticks with what is right and what can be done, and stays away from what is not right or what cannot be done.

3. Finally, notice that different kinds of organizations can have different collections of criteria for measuring their vitality and performance. These criteria may be deeply rooted in people's minds. For instance, in sizing up a business organization, people tend to use industry attractiveness and firm strength as two major criteria. The following lists summarize the sub-criteria within the major criteria for evaluating a corporation. The list can serve as another means for studying corporate HD and strategic position.

INDUSTRY ATTRACTIVENESS FACTORS

1. Market Factors
- Type: Size of the market, volume, region served, degree of vertical integration, volatility of market sales, cyclical nature.
- Growth Prospects: Stage of product life cycle, projected future growth rate, past growth.
- Characteristics: Distribution system, brand differentiation, price sensitivity, captive customers, necessity/luxury product.

2. Competitive Factors
- Industry concentration: Current concentration index, projected change in concentration.
- Entry barrier/exit barrier: Capital requirements, product differentiation, economies of scale, distribution channels, brand identity, switching costs, access to raw material.
- Buyer power: Number of buyers, switching costs, dependence on industry.
- Supplier power: Number of suppliers, dependence on industry, switching costs.
- Threats of substitutes: Price/performance tradeoff.
- Overseas competitors: Number of major foreign players, cost factors (factor costs differences), technology availability in other countries.
- Rivalry among competitors: Number of competitors, industry capacity vs. demand, diversity of competition, degree of product differentiation.

3. Financial Factors
- Cost factors: Raw materials, wages and salaries, fixed vs. variable costs, selling expenses.
- Efficiency factors: Learning curve effects, economies of scale, average inventory levels, productivity, capacity utilization.

- Capital structure: Industry average leverage ratio, average (price/earning) ratio, trends.
- Financial results: Past profitability, future profit potential, share price trends.

4. Socio-Political Factors

- Government and legal: Consistency of government policies, antitrust laws, regulation/deregulation, EPA requirements, equal opportunity requirements, fair trade decisions, consumer protection, trade laws.
- Social attitude and trends: Changes in consumer preferences, demographics shifts, changes in population mix.
- Outside stakeholders influence: Relationship and support, impact on decision making.
- Labor issues: Availability of skills, degree of unionization, attitude, motivation level.

5. Technological Factors

- Complexity: Skills required, investment intensity, volatility, availability, changes in technology.
- Product innovation and development: Basic R&D requirements, applied R&D requirements, importance of patent position, rate of technological advancement.
- Productivity: Degree of automation, work force attitude.

FIRM STRENGTHS FACTORS

1. Market Factors

- Company type: Geographical area served, degree of vertical integration, volatility and cyclical firm sales, breadth of product line, location of plants.
- Prospects: Size, growth rate relative to industry.
- Company characteristics: Effectiveness of distribution network, relationship with dealers, brand differentiation, advertising and promotional skills, sales force effectiveness, captive customers, vulnerability to changes in demand, perceived quality of products.

2. Competitive Factors

- Company dominance: Market share (domestic), market

share (overseas), changes in market share.
- Exit barriers: Capital investment, resale value of equipment/assets, number of employees involved, community pressure.
- Bargaining power of buyer on firm: Number of buyers, fragmented/concentrated, buyer switching costs.
- Bargaining power of supplier on firm: Number of suppliers, size relative to suppliers, dependence of suppliers on firm.
- Vulnerability to competition: Number of major domestic competitors, number of foreign competitors, basis of competition.

3. Organization and Management
- Management quality: Top management, leadership, quality of strategic decisions, middle/functional management, availability of general management skills.
- Management style: Proactive/reactive, risk taking propensity, participative/autocratic, aggressive/passive, flexible/inflexible, external/internal focus.
- Management loyalty/morale: Turnover, tenure in the organization, commitment to the organization.
- Organizational culture: Shared values and norms, company policies, procedures, attitudes.
- Systems: Information & control systems, organization structure, reward and evaluation systems.
- Personnel: Background, skills.

4. Financial Factors
- Cost structure: Overhead/total cost, cost of raw materials, wages and salaries, sales cost/total sales.
- Achieved efficiency: Decrease in cost/unit achieved, collection period-receivables.
- Capital structure: Debt/equity, ability to raise equity, borrowing capacity, distribution of shares.
- Financial performance: Stock price and changes, price/earning ratio, profitability (return on investment or return on equity), stability of profits, reserves, cash flows.

5. Socio-Political Factors
- Government and legal: Firm's ability to adapt/cope with

change, firm's ability to influence, compliance with regulatory bodies, impact of regulations, position adopted on important issues.
• Social attitudes and trends: Impact of social changes on firm, adaptability to change, proactive moves to take advantage of opportunities.
• Outside stakeholders: Influence of outside stakeholders on strategies and decisions, extent of stakeholder support, relationship with stakeholders.
• Labor issues: Influence of organized labor, attitude of labor.

6. Technological Factors
• Technological complexity: Size of investment, skills availability, available technological know-how, technological follower/leader.
• Products innovation and development: Patents available, new product capabilities, R & D facilities.
• Productivity: Work force attitude, degree of automation of the firm, output/employee ratio, inventory turnover ratio, capacity utilization, economies of scale, inventory levels compared to industry average, capacity utilization, age of plant and equipment.

WORKSHEET #1:
HABITUAL DOMAIN EXPANDER ...Things To Do
WEEK: _____
AWARENESS AND IMPROVEMENT RECORD

EVENTS	TIME ALLOCATED	IMPROVEMENTS	NOTES	% OF TOTAL TIME
Primary Jobs and Job-Related Activities				
Social Missions and Works				
Health and Illness				
Events with Intimates				
Family Events and Problems				
Hobbies and Pursuits of Special Interests				
Religion, the Great Nature and the Universe				

AWARENESS AND IMPROVEMENT RECORD

ROLES PLAYED	TIME IN ROLE	EXAMPLE SITUATIONS	% OF TOTAL TIME
Official Role			
Implicit			
Insider			
Outsider			
Superior			
Equal			
Inferior			
Teacher			
Student			
Principle Player			
Cheerleader			
Representative			
Mediator			

WORKSHEET #2:
HABITUAL DOMAIN EXPANDER
TIMETABLE

DATE: _____

8 :
9 :
10 :
11 :
12 :
1 :
2 :
3 :
4 :
5 :
6 :
7 :
8 :
9 :
10 :
11 :

PRIORITY/TO DO

( ) _____
( ) _____
( ) _____
( ) _____
( ) _____
( ) _____
( ) _____
( ) _____

HD PRINCIPLES TO USE TODAY

_____
_____
_____
_____
_____
_____
_____

SITUATIONS I APPLIED HD TO

_____
_____
_____
_____
_____
_____
_____

SPECIFIC RESULTS, CHANGES AND NOTES

_____
_____
_____
_____
_____
_____
_____

Index

About the Author

P.L. Yu created Habitual Domains, his system for achieving success in life and in business, from a broad base of knowledge grounded in both Eastern and Western thought, science and practice. Raised in Taiwan and further educated in the United States, Dr. Yu is recognized around the world as a remarkable thinker, scholar, teacher and advisor to business.

Since 1977, he has held an endowed chair as the Carl A. Scupin Distinguished Professor at the University of Kansas School of Business, and he is an internationally sought after lecturer. He advises businesses in the East and West on management issues, especially in operations and strategic decision-making.

In addition, Dr. Yu is a martial arts master. He has studied and practiced Kung Fu since 1954, and his specialties include Tai Ghee (太極), Form and Will (形意), Bar Kwa (八卦), and Shao Lin (少林). He is currently the faculty advisor and instructor for the University of Kansas Kung Fu Club.

He has won awards for his teaching and research. He is the area editor for *Operations Research* in the areas of decision analysis, bargaining and negotiation, and an associate editor for the *Journal of Optimization Theory and Applications*. He has published seven books and more than 80 professional articles.

P.L. Yu graduated from the National Taiwan University in 1963 and received his Ph.D. in operations research and industrial engineering from Johns Hopkins University in 1969. Before taking his position at the University of Kansas, he taught at the University of Rochester and the University of Texas at Austin. His research interests range from mathematically sophisticated areas such as optimal controls, differential games and mathematical programming, to areas related to human behavior, such as management, psychology and philosophy. His publications address multiple criteria decision making, optimal design, optimal control, differential games, systems science in psychology and philosophy and — of course — habitual domains.

A Highwater Editions book

Editor:	Jane Mobley, Ph.D.
Textual Editors:	Robert Butler
	Michael DeMent
	Paul Peterson
	Beth Scalet
	Lyn Foister
Art Director:	Vivian Strand
Production Artist:	Jeane Counard
Administrator:	Joi Kara Jenkins
Author's Assistant:	Unkei Chong
Photographers:	Roy Inman: i, xvi, xxiv, 30, 38, 54, 62, 66, 70, 96, 124, 128, 152, 154, 156
	Joe Parker: 4, 51, 86, 102, 132

Translations of selections from Confucius and original poems "Tai Ghee" (p. 124), "Wisdom" (p. 46-47) and "Bright and Positive Mentality" (p. 167-168) are by Po-Lung Yu, Ph.D.